TRANSPARENT
See

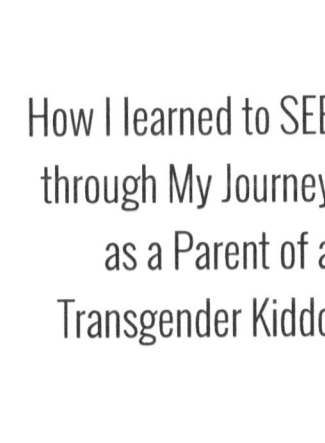

How I learned to SEE
through My Journey
as a Parent of a
Transgender Kiddo

BY MEAGAN SCHULTZ SKIDMORE

Cover Art by AJ Skidmore

TRANSPARENT See

How I learned to SEE through My Journey
as a Parent of a Transgender Kiddo
Copyright © 2025 by Meagan Schultz Skidmore

To request permissions, contact the publisher
at publish@joapublishing.com.

Hardcover ISBN: 978-1-967575-20-6
Paperback ISBN: 978-1-967575-21-3
eBook ISBN: 978-1-967575-22-0
Printed in the USA.

Joan of Arc Publishing
Meridian, ID 83646
www.joapublishing.com

Enjoy Your Bonus Workbook!

Thank you for reading *TransparentSEE*.
As a special gift, I've created a bonus workbook designed
to help you go deeper with the concepts in this book.

How to Access Your Workbook

Simply scan the QR code below with your phone to
unlock your workbook:

TransparentSEE

TABLE OF
CONTENTS

TESTIMONIALS

I've had the joy of meeting Meagan Skidmore multiple times— and even appearing on her podcast—so I can say firsthand that her passion and the work she's doing are nothing short of incredible. In TransparentSEE, Meagan invites us into her world as the mother of a trans [kiddo], navigating faith, identity, and fierce love in a conservative setting. With rare vulnerability, she shares the heart-wrenching and hope-filled moments that shaped her awakening.

What makes TransparentSEE so powerful is Meagan's unique gift: she doesn't just tell her story—she helps us gently peel back the layers of our own. Through raw honesty, spiritual insight, and unwavering compassion, she teaches us to break free from confining boxes and begin seeing with our truest vision. This book isn't just for queer parents or faith communities—it's a courageous call for anyone longing to live more authentically, with love at the center.

If you've met Meagan or experienced her humanity and warmth, you know that TransparentSEE will guide us through uncertainty with grace, help us hold space for ourselves and others, and remind us that sometimes, love asks us to see again.

Sara Cunningham, *Founder of Free Mom Hugs*

TransparentSEE is a beautiful extended reflection of a mother learning to see the true nature of love through her experience coming to love a child just as they were created. Meagan walks her readers through her own journey of awakening in a way that invites each of us to know what love truly is. This book is honest, vulnerable, and raw. It speaks into the beauty of what relationships can be when we allow others to flower just as they are--not as we think they need to be. I highly recommend this book.

Valerie Hamaker, LPC, *Latter Day Struggles* Podcast

It was relatable, vulnerable, but also strong and confident. I appreciated how she interwove memories, journal writing, stories and insights from her work as a life coach. Understanding her experiences as a woman of faith, mother of a trans child and human was validating and refreshing. I recommend LDS parents of a trans child and LDS leaders read this book. I thank Meagan for doing the work to love her child, transform as a person, and share her journey with the world!

Dr. Julia Campbell Bernards,
parent of 4 amazing kids, three of whom are LGBTQ+
identifying

ACKNOWLEDGMENTS

I volunteered to be coached in our regular MOSAI network meeting. Jeff was there leading the session. It was an emotional day; I had recently dropped my kiddo off to start freshman year at NAU. I was exhausted.

I remember saying something like, "Sometimes, I just don't know where my kiddo gets his strength from."

Jeff asked me, thoughtfully and calmly, "Can you see that he gets it from you?"

No. Until that moment, I could not.

Thank you for teaching me Keira, Juliet, Jeff, Nathan, Glenn, Brooke, Trish, Bailey, Mike, Zeljka, JOA, and all members of the MOSAI Network, and for believing in me and supporting me.

And to my coaches for the most transformational breakthrough sessions: Sarah Trapkus, Minda Pacheco, Lindsay Poelman, and Kim Job.

TransparentSEE

PROLOGUE

"One day you will tell your story of how you've overcome what you're going through now, and it will become part of someone else's survival guide."

~ Anonymous

For as long as I can remember, I have had dreams and visions of me talking to large crowds, standing on a stage or some other place, speaking my truth.

Maybe it was a figment of my imagination.

Maybe it was a premonition of things to come.

Perhaps it is something I felt called to do, and keeping it within my dreamscape felt more safe.

Regardless, at this point in my journey, I believe that crossing paths with my publisher, mentor, book-medium badass, and now friend, Keira Brinton, was zero coincidence.

Anyone can hire a publisher; however, God-the Universe-Divinity knew I needed a gentle nudging (translation: a big, huge, kick in the butt) to get my story out. Even as I place finishing touches on this copy before sending it to our editor, Mindy, I feel the shakes coming on, and tears threaten to fall down my cheek. I even played OM chanting at 417 Hz to remove negative blocks and calm my nerves.

It will never *not* be a bit scary or nerve-racking to put my truth out into the world. And this, by far, is the most significant way I have done so to date.

I believe my connection with Keira of Joan of Arc Publishing, and subsequently the MOSAI Network, is the reason you are now holding this book in your hands.

As you read, may your story now be intertwined with mine.

May you feel the tapestry of human connection tightly woven into your soul, together not just with mine but all of humanity.

This is the real, the raw, the ugly, the beautiful, the candid, the thoughtful, the bold, and the scared as sh*t.

This is me.

When you read, you may love me, you may hate me, you may relate to me, you may judge me, you may reject me, or you may resonate with me. I'm OK with all of that because at the end of the day, peeling back the layers and being unapologetically, authentically me is what I have come to value the most.

Even if everything is at risk and my voice shakes. Or maybe *especially when.*

More than anything, my biggest wish is that you feel my sincerity, love, and open arms as I give you a porthole view into my heart. This is the most flyingest fly-on-the-wall view into my world I have ever allowed to be witnessed.

Let the journey commence.

INTRODUCTION

"Love freely given has no beginning or end."

~ Anonymous

Trying hard to reach out
But when I tried to speak out
Felt like no one could hear me
Wanted to belong here
But something felt so wrong here
So I prayed (I would pray)
I could break away

I'll spread my wings and I'll learn how to fly
I'll do what it takes 'til I touch the sky
And I'll make a wish, take a chance, make a change
And break away
Out of the darkness and into the sun
But I won't forget all the ones that I love
I'll take a risk, take a chance, make a change
And break away

~ "Breakaway," recorded by Kelly Clarkson,
written by Matthew Gerrard, Bridget Benenate,
and Avril Lavigne.

1

In 2019, I was searching for answers. I was in more emotional, mental, and spiritual pain than I had ever experienced. I had new information, and I knew my life was never going to be the same. In my search for answers, I remember coming across a blog post that read something like this:

> *Imagine sitting in church on Sunday with your family all lined up in a pew.*
>
> *You look around; people are smiling, enjoying the speaker. The mom in front of you is braiding her daughter's hair. You can hear the toddler behind you screaming for a snack.*
>
> *And before you know what hits, the ground starts shaking, and an earthquake rips through your temple and leaves this gigantic hole right in your pew where your family is sitting. You're injured, you're bleeding, you're in need of a triage. You look around, searching for help.*
>
> *And that's when it stuns you to realize your pew was the only one that was hit.*
>
> *Everybody else around you is carrying on like nothing happened.*

This story resonated with me because that is how I felt upon learning that my youngest child, age thirteen at the time, identified as LGBTQIA+. I come from a conservative faith background—the LDS faith—born and raised just like my parents, just like their parents and their parents' parents.

I knew the tenets of my faith. I had been taught how to think and what to believe about LGBTQIA+ individuals: it wasn't OK for a person to be LGBTQIA+, it was a choice, it was an abomination, it was sinful—especially to act on it—even to the point that it would keep them, and possibly their families, from living with God in what we believe to be the next life or the next step of progression.

This thought absolutely petrified me. I thought, *Surely we can figure out a way for my kiddo to fit into this heteronormative box.* Because, you see, I knew all about checking boxes.

I had checked many in my own life. I was born in the faith. I was baptized at eight. At twelve, I entered the youth program. I was president of many of my youth classes. I learned Spanish and served a Spanish-speaking mission.

I was married in one of the LDS temples—the highest place of worship—and then started a family. The thought of not checking this box of eternal family was something I could not bear.

The cognitive dissonance was absolutely overwhelming. I felt my soul ripping apart, pulled in polar opposite directions between two things that I deeply cared about. It nearly broke me.

I remember one day while walking down the stairs in our home, I was paralyzed.

I was paralyzed with fear.

I couldn't breathe.

I quietly prayed aloud, "I don't know what's going on. I don't know what I'm doing. I don't know what's next.

I'm scared. I feel lost. Help me, please."

And almost immediately, I felt this blanket of peace settle over me as I received a very clear message to slow down, to see the child in front of me the way God sees them, to focus on their heart, to see their soul. This was the beginning of God taking my heart that had been broken wide open and giving it a makeover.

What was it for? Was it just performative? What good are external boxes if it hadn't affected me internally? Because after all, it's what's on the inside that counts, right? How many times have I said that or heard that over the years?

Over the next days, weeks, months, years, God changed my heart. I began walking through a refiner's fire—"began to" because this is an ongoing process—as I began to *see* folks: my kiddo and others—not their hair or clothes, or their tattoos, piercings, earrings, or material possessions.

Instead, I began to see their hearts. I began to see beautiful souls, fellow children of this gigantic family of God. I began to see the divinity that already exists within each one. And I believe I began to see them more like God would—for their talents, abilities, strengths, weaknesses, joys, sorrows, characteristics—as they go through this journey. I learned that queer folks were forcing me to lean into discomfort and reexamine some very long held beliefs.

My "capital P" Purpose is not to convince you to be or do or think the way that I am, do, or think but rather to inspire you to consider:

- What are your boxes?
- Do you like them?
- Are they serving you, or are they just performative?
- Did you choose them?
- Do you even remember choosing them? How are they getting in the way of your "capital P" Purpose, your "capital C" Calling?

In my work, I help clients with three things. First, I help them to recognize the stories they've been telling themselves that have contributed to the identity they've been carrying with them their entire lives. Second, we identify their core values. When your world has been rocked, you have to establish an aligned center from which to lead, taking leaps of faith and making those big decisions that you're so used to somebody else making for you. And finally, we process emotions. Lots of big, scary, sometimes ugly emotions come up in this process, and that's OK. Emotions aren't to be feared, pushed down, or avoided. Emotions are our teachers. They show us where we've been and where we're at and can direct us where we need to go. I help my clients look inward, heal their inner child, and give that child what it never received.

Before I could begin to help others, I first had to do this for myself. I learned to identify my stories, name my core values, and listen to my emotions and then allow them to teach me and direct me in my next steps on this pathway (that didn't even exist yet).

Ironically, the journey of being a parent of an LGBTQIA+ child helped me begin to heal my own inner child and offer it what it had not received.

TransparentSEE

TRANSPARENTSEE
(definition)

The act or process of transmutation, or changing the state of being into another form through peeling back the layers with a willingness to be open with your kids, showing them how to "do life" even if—and when—you make mistakes, allowing yourself to be taught by the next generation.

In my experience, when I do this with my kids, our relationship and trust deepens and grows beautifully in ways it may not have otherwise. My kids have taught me to be truly authentic, or in other words, emotionally, mentally, and spiritually transparent.

To be authentic means, by default, vulnerability is along for the ride—like it or not. Embracing, let alone leaning into, vulnerability is not something humans run toward.

Adults can't imagine the courage it takes for a teen to lean into vulnerability as they attempt to find and honor their true self and identity. I think adults have forgotten because they tend to walk around with masks on. For adults and teens alike, surrendering and submitting to authenticity in hopes of finding belonging means risking much. But for teens especially, at such a young age, social capital is everything; my child risked it all and did experience loss. And this set us on a journey of searching for and finding belonging, peace, and love—not just mere tolerance.

Why?

Nobody should have to settle for tolerance. We all long to be loved and desire to be seen for who we are in our core being. What does it even mean to be "seen"? It means being

- listened to,
- heard,
- believed,
- honored,
- embraced,
- celebrated,
- having no conditions placed,
- loved *for who you are*, not in spite of, and
- having a seat at the table (no maybes or speaking metaphorically— an actual seat at the actual table).

I am a completely transformed soul because of my transgender son, and I would. not. change. anything. I treasure my increase in knowledge, deepened understanding, and expanded ability to love bigger because of my associations with friends and loved ones who are transgender.

I no longer seek for external cues to inform and define myself and others. My eyes have been opened, and

I see humans.

I see hearts.

I see souls.

1

TRANSMISSION
(send from one person/place to another)

When all of my days are done
Of pleasin' everyone
I'll finally have begun

Our time on Earth ain't gon' last forever
I'm on my journey and I won't be afraid
No more confusion and aggravation
What is this life for? I'm gonna win

I'm gonna live my truth in this life
I am not gonna live a lie
'Cause I came here to be alive
I am here to be human

I'm gonna keep my head to the sky
Gonna walk each step with pride
'Cause I came here to be alive
I am here to be human

When I'm free to shine my light
I'm ready to take flight
The past is out of sight

I'm on the move and I shall endeavor
No one is perfect and I won't be ashamed
My heart's yearning for transformation
What is this life for? I'm gonna win"

~ "Human,"
Written and recorded by Lenny Kravitz

In September of 2020, I began my coaching certification through the Life Coach School. A month later, I decided to create a social media account to coincide with this new journey. It didn't take me long to feel the pangs of vulnerability hangovers as I began to post openly. I had childlike hopes my shares would reflect this new journey while simultaneously helping me cultivate my new persona of life coach.

In November of the same year, I committed to myself to showing up authentically and truthfully regardless of what others around me were doing or saying, or not doing or saying. I decided to purposely do this for myself, not just on social media but in all other aspects of life.

I learned I could feel the jitters at the same time that I was feeling peaceful assurance that what I was speaking or sharing was good and right. I could be shaking—literally, physically shaking—and hit the "submit" button with a knowing that resonated and dropped so deep in my soul I couldn't question its presence. It left an unmistakable, soft residue of peace each time.

I didn't know it at the time, but the more I went through these motions to share either personally or virtually, the more profoundly I was cultivating a relationship of trust with myself. I was deepening a relationship with someone who already existed but that I hadn't really taken the chance or had the opportunity to know. And this person was the real me.

The real you exists already. You may not have met the real you, but it is there deep inside your heart and soul. Or perhaps the real you is already tapping from inside your heart, begging to be seen, allowed to breathe, and set free.

You know the sensation of this tapping. You have met it before. It is found whispered in wishes when blowing out birthday candles as a child. It comes in the form of dreams of what you would be when you grew up. It is that tug on your heartstrings, or that push-pull of energy felt by your spirit when you ethereally connect with other human beings.

This is the real you communicating in a way that words fail to describe, vying for your attention in an effort to be seen, heard, acknowledged, or validated. It continues to try until the keeper of this beating heart consciously or unconsciously puts a stop to the gentle nudging.

Outside pressures, societal messaging, or family expectations can translate into individual narratives, beliefs, and expectations. Often these are not authentic to the real you, and coercing them is ultimately what pulls the plug on the nudging, that beautiful, exquisite, life-giving force.

In real time, ignoring the real you deep inside looks like repression, masking, dodging, and lying to self or others, all of which flies in the face of authenticity. Without authentic living, a person will die a slow death, even though they have a pulse that registers on a monitor. Let me rephrase: without authentic living, a person already IS dying a slow death—a death of self, of hopes, of dreaming.

Notice I didn't say "death of *dreams.*" One must allow themselves to go through the *practice of dreaming* before landing on actual hopes and dreams. If your authentic self is stifled, so, too, will be your dreaming and dreams.

Along with all of your dreams, the real you is hidden behind walls: perfectionism, shame, control, "performing" for others to please them or gain validation for yourself. Like turpentine to oil paints, authenticity is the key to dissolving the figurative mortar that will slowly but surely deconstruct the walls brick by brick. Living authentically is the only way for this to happen; there will be no more hiding behind walls. And this is a good thing. It is the natural course of things. Once the wall is down, the real you will continue to open up and bloom even more.

Synonymous to authenticity are truth, genuineness, integrity, originality, honesty, openness, realness. Starting in 2019, living authentically became a necessity as I pivoted in my faith journey. What I now call a faith expansion began when I struggled to reconcile elements of my faith of origin: LDS (also known as Mormon). I could not hold the inherent tension that exists between two seemingly opposing concepts—or in my case, doctrine—and then lie to myself about it. Authenticity was the only way forward.

I had to acknowledge that the tenets of my faith regarding LGBTQIA+ individuals and my own personal, lived experience as a parent of an LGBTQIA+ kiddo were in complete opposition. If I were to continue to move forward as a thinking, feeling, breathing human being, I could not lie to myself about this and what I was experiencing and being taught, from within and by that Source of truth greater than us all. Authentically living is what ultimately saved my life—spiritually, mentally, and otherwise.

I have learned how living and expressing self authentically is a true source of hope. And is that not what we are taught? To live with hope? As a seventh generation Mormon, I was taught:

"Therefore, ye must press forward with a steadfastness in Christ, having a perfect brightness of hope, and a love of God and of all men" 2 Nephi 31:20, *The Book of Mormon*.

As a lifelong member—complete with having attended seminary through all four years of high school and served a full-time mission—I knew my scriptures. And yet, I was not finding "a perfect brightness of hope" at the intersection of teachings passed down to me and the real-life experience of those in the LGBTQIA+ community. To have a perfect brightness of hope means to see things from a curious lens that allows for questions and doubts. Questions and doubts invite the possibility of MORE—additional—what else's and possibilities! And yet, within my faith, family, and community, finding this approach being modeled was uncommon. I decided part of living authentically, of listening to the real me inside, was to live with this curious lens of expansion.

The word *expansion* evokes a sense of hope simply by definition: it means bigger, greater, larger. I like to picture a hot air balloon as the heat from the fire causes surrounding air to warm and fill the balloon. The air warms, and the molecules quicken and move faster, causing the balloon to expand and rise. The warm air literally expands until it fills every corner and pocket of the inside of the balloon. Once those are filled, the balloon doesn't stop expanding there. The movement of the molecules expands so greatly that they cause the balloon to separate from the earth and take flight. As long as the heat stokes the fire, that balloon continues to rise and move on its journey, exploring uncharted territory, experiencing and learning of things previously unknown to the balloon and its occupants.

Talk about EXPANSIVE.

In this symbolic process of transmission—the act of transferring something from one place to another—the balloon is expansive. The people inside, the warm air, the balloon itself—all embody expansion.

At dictionary.com, the words "transmit" and "transmission" come from the Latin word *transmittere*, a combination of the preposition *trans*—"across or beyond"—and the verb—*mittere* "to let go or to send."

Through the process of writing this book, I am symbolically letting go of things in the past that no longer serve me while simultaneously sending out into the universe that which I have learned in this process. This book is my transmission, or my message of expansion. I could say that to personally embody this expansion, I've *had* to become more transparent, vulnerable, and authentic on my journey; however, it feels more accurate to say that *I've chosen to be so.*

It is at once terrifying and fulfilling. Ironically, it is through this part of the journey that I've been able to cultivate more hope: the hope of an authentic journey, exploring uncharted territory, and integrating the learning from the experiences of things unknown with those already known.

It is my sincere hope that you will receive my transmission.

2.

TRANSFERENCE
(carry it across)

I don't know what I've been livin' on, but
It's not enough to fill me up
I need more than just words can say
I need everything this life can give me
Hey, hey, yeah
'Cause sometimes is not enough
Aw!

Come on, baby, close your eyes, let go
This can be everything we've dreamed
It's not work that makes it work on
Now let the magic do the work for you, yes, honey

'Cause something reached out and touched me
Now I know all I want

I want the best of both worlds
And, honey, I know what it's worth
If we could have the best of both worlds
We'd have Heaven right here on Earth, ooh

———

Whoa, you don't have to die and go to heaven
Or hang around to be born again
Just tune in to what this place has got to offer
'Cause we may never be here again, aw!

I want the best of both worlds
Honey, I know what it's worth
If we could have the best of both worlds
A little Heaven right here on Earth, come on

~ "Best of Both Worlds,"
written and recorded by Van Halen
(Sammy Hagar, Edward Van Halen,
Alex Van Halen, and Michael Anthony).

Just outside of Flagstaff, Arizona, up toward the San Francisco Peaks, is the largest ponderosa pine forest in the world. It's here I dropped off my youngest kiddo, my transgender son, for his freshman year of college at Northern Arizona University.

There is nothing like the smell of layers and layers of dried pine needles blanketing the ground. I helped him move in the week before classes started, then on the first day of classes, I decided to take a short hike just below Mars Hill Trail. It was a much needed diversion from all the emotion bubbling up inside of me.

A million pinecones dotted the space, mixed with wildflowers, tall forest grass, and an assortment of rocks sized pebble to boulder that were sprinkled about. The smell of the pine forest instantly takes me many years back to my younger days when a different me existed, one whose ghost lingers but no longer pulses through the blood in my veins.

So many questions . . .

Is it OK to be who I am now?

Have I lost something along this pathway I've taken?

If so, what have I lost along the way?

What have I gained?

Am I going to regret it?

Have I made a big mistake?

Mind you, the "mistake" I'm questioning has nothing to do with leaving my child at NAU for his freshman year. I'm referring to the evolution of who I have become along the way: learning to become his mother, the mom he *needs* me to be, not the mom my upbringing taught me was "the only" way to be a mom, to be an individual, to be a person of faith.

So my feelings are a mixture: bitter and sweet, sad and elated, wistful and hopeful all at the same time. And let me tell you, those are big feelings that I hadn't been prepared for, especially for them to burst like a shaken can of soda and explode into my atmosphere! I have felt somewhat lacking in trying to metabolize them, feel them, welcome them, learn from, and thank them as I leave them behind so I can move forward, above and beyond—transcending them.

There are so many ways to parent. To deny the myriad ways that exist to care for and meet the needs of another human being is to live in a box or even a cage.

It is to live in a non-reality.

This is dangerous because it leads to death . . .

Death of human spirit, death of emotional intimacy, death of personal growth for parent and child. Unfortunately, this has the potential to leave a strain on relationships or make it so that you miss out on the child altogether. You literally don't see *the person*.

Living inside a proverbial cage blinds us. This isn't lyrical hyperbole; we cannot see what we *can't* see. And therein lies the tragedy.

We have to allow judgment-free observation, unconditional compassion, and unbiased inquisitiveness—all things that we were born with and engaged in wholeheartedly during childhood. Unless we choose to engage in those in our adulthood, we remain enclosed in and blinded by that cage. Observation, compassion, and inquisitiveness are the keys that unlock the door of the cage.

Only when it's unlocked can we step outside and leave, then begin experiencing the freedom that comes from choosing our thoughts, owning our viewpoints, and taking a breath of fresh air as we explore and eventually embrace the unknown, even if and when we goof up. I don't like to call things "mistakes." I choose to see them as life lessons that teach us.

To leave the cage is a new lease on life. What does that mean, anyway, "a new lease on life"?

While on my hike, I was recalling the many earlier versions of me, ones that held different values, had different viewpoints, saw through different lenses, and used a different compass. When the compass you were given through the religious foundation upon which you've relied your entire life is no longer calibrated to your true north, life gets pretty scary.

If I was to physically, spiritually, mentally, and emotionally survive the earthquake (see "Introduction"), I had no choice but to find a new compass. Did it include the same cardinal points? Did I discard some or bring in new ones? Perhaps I was to learn to navigate these points with a new spin on orienteering, adding and taking away as I went seeking and discovering. I was about to find out.

To create my compass, I had to rely on the Inner Voice I had come to know very well throughout my life. If there is one thing that I was certain of, it's that I knew what it was like to "hear" and then carry out the impressions that came to me. Some refer to it as personal revelation. Others call it a download. Regardless of the vocabulary words used to describe it, I felt very directed by Divine guidance.

Transference means "carry it across." How do you carry it across? How do you evaluate something you've understood a certain way your entire life, re-view it—literally, "re" + "view" it (look at it through a different lens)—and then decide what to bring with you moving forward, or "carry it across?"

I'll share what I have tried and continue to try.

Most of us think we know what matters most. You may even believe you know what you personally value the most. Name your top five core values in ten seconds. I bet you can't do it!

Some can, most can't. If I gave you a list of one hundred values, it would take you a week to narrow it down to five. Growing up in a conservative faith, my values were selected for me: faith, Divine Nature, individual worth, knowledge, choice and accountability, good works, and integrity. When they were first introduced to me in the LDS Young Women's Program when I was almost thirteen years of age, I wasn't entirely sure what all of them meant. But I dove into the program with gusto and intended to learn all about and develop them.

Those seven values served me well and laid a fine foundation. In fact, they are what have carried me through these past years as my faith foundations have been rocked. Faith in myself and in the Divine Nature I (and we all) have planted the embryonic seeds of my faith journey decades ago. I still return to this faith.

As we grow and evolve, so do our values. Identifying our core values becomes a compass guiding us north, south, east, and west. Knowing our core values creates a moral foundation, a solid foundation upon which to stand and move forward. Doing so puts us in alignment in mind, body, and soul.

I have come to learn that we must identify our core values, and that process of identification goes in cycles. What is most important to you right now may be different in a year; as we evolve and change, so do our core values. That is not a good thing or a bad thing. It's just a thing.

In the process of narrowing down your core values you begin to see your own, custom-made value compass take shape. Scan the QR code at the end of the chapter to use my Determine Your Values Guide to help you narrow down your core values.

Here's mine:

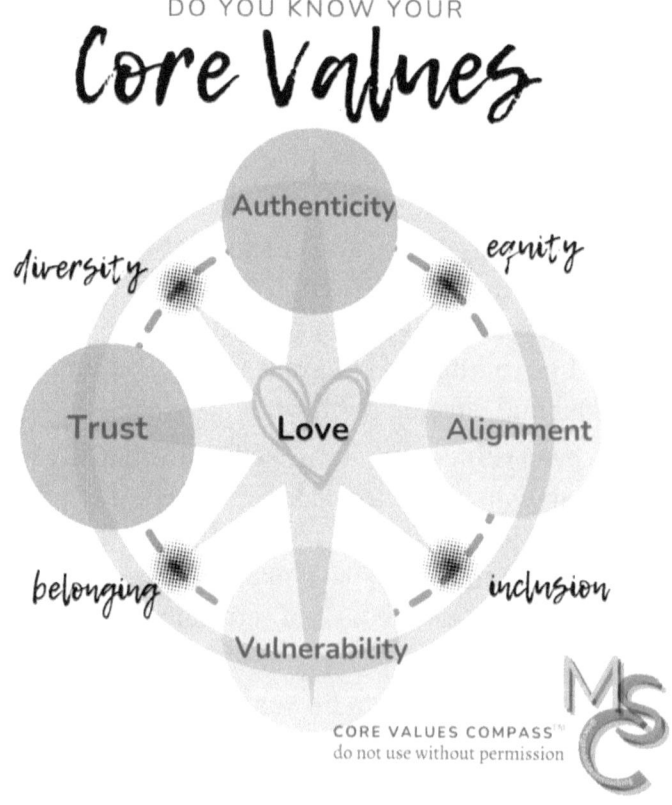

DO YOU KNOW YOUR

Core Values

CORE VALUES COMPASS
do not use without permission

When faced with choices that were once made for me—what to wear, what to eat, what to believe, or what to say—I run the choice through this "filter" of my values compass. I ask myself if it fits within my N, S, E, and W compass points: does it allow me to be authentic, does it invite vulnerability, can I remain in my integrity and personal alignment, and does it foster and cultivate trust in both myself and others? It makes for almost seamless transitioning from a high demand, choices-made-for-you background to one of autonomy.

Once you've determined your core values, consider asking yourself these two questions that were offered to me by my esteemed coach and mentor Trudi Lebron:

1. What do my values ask of me? (This will give you hints at your life's Purpose.)

2. What would I do if I radically centered myself on my core values? (This often hints at your life's Mission.)

You can also consider expansion values. I have mine positioned on the northeast, southeast, southwest, and northwest points on my compass. For me, diversity, equity, inclusion, and belonging (DEIB) are paramount. They are expansive by nature, leaving room for improvement and growth. Having them as part of my values compass is nonnegotiable. If someone or something ignores these key points on my values compass, I move on. I seek after causes and support initiatives that aim to create DEIB.

Now, all that remains then is to follow your values. Do them. Live your life in alignment with them. Embody them. Make choices based on and not outside of your core values. You will find a power and strength like never before.

Today, I carry across with me the things that an earlier version of me was taught, that I still value, that still have meaning and bring joy to me. The rest I can thank for the experience and learning they offered and then let them go with grace, gratitude, and hope. And with my values compass in hand, I look toward the future.

This is transference.

3

TRANSLUCENCE

(allowing light to pass through diffusely; spread out, not directed in one place)

You with the sad eyes
Don't be discouraged
Oh I realize
It's hard to take courage
In a world full of people
You can lose sight of it all
And the darkness inside you
Can make you feel so small

But I see your true colors
Shining through
I see your true colors
And that's why I love you
So don't be afraid to let them show
Your true colors
True colors are beautiful
Like a rainbow

Show me a smile then
Don't be unhappy, can't remember
When I last saw you laughing
If this world makes you crazy
And you've taken all you can bear
You call me up
Because you know I'll be there

And I'll see your true colors
Shining through
I see your true colors
And that's why I love you
So don't be afraid to let it show
Your true colors
True colors are beautiful
Like a rainbow

If this world makes you crazy
And you've taken all you can bear
You call me up
Because you know I'll be there

And I'll see your true colors
Shining through
I see your true colors
And that's why I love you
So don't be afraid to let it show

Your true colors
True colors
True colors
Shining through

I see your true colors
And that's why I love you

So don't be afraid to let them show
Your true colors
True colors are beautiful
Like a rainbow

~ "True Colors,"
recorded by Cyndi Lauper,
written by Billy Steinberg and Tom Kelly

When we are young it's normal, and even expected, that our faith, beliefs, and practice look quite alike among us. Growing up, I was taught certain things—given boxes to check, if you will—akin to my siblings, neighbors, friends, and loved ones. In some ways, the outcome was to become carbon copies, though that wasn't explicitly stated. There was no mal intention; I believe those who come before us actually have our best interests at heart.

Here's the big BUT. . . .

But what happens when we mature physically, spiritually, emotionally, and mentally and try to allow our personal growth to take the natural path it wants to follow?

Nobody comes between me and my spirituality.

I was not always able to say those words and mean them *and* feel safe in my body. It took many tries, much questioning, and many tears, going back and forth between thoughts of, *am I losing myself?* and *am I finding myself?* and thinking it could be possible to find and connect with God in and of myself. What I was experiencing, thinking, and feeling were different from what I was taught I *should have* been experiencing, thinking, and feeling. My soul was trying to emerge and reflect on the outside who I already was and am on the inside.

I was struggling to differentiate. You see, differentiation of self is not something that was taught to nor cultivated in me in my faith of origin. Nor was it for my parents or their parents. I am pointing no blame.

It took having a child come out as transgender to teach me what *is* possible. In terms of biology, to differentiate into something means "to develop into a cell or tissue that has a specialized structure or function. [For example] stem cells can differentiate into many types of other cells."[1]

What this definition doesn't explicitly state but certainly implies is that all the cells start out looking very much alike. The reason cell differentiation is so important is that it allows medical professionals to target the cancerous ones before they divide and continue growing to advanced stages.

Looking at differentiation through a sociological lens gives insight into its role within family and other systems. According to bowencenter.org, "a person with a well-differentiated 'self' recognizes [their] realistic dependence on others, but can stay calm and clear headed enough in the face of conflict."[2]

Differentiation was not a word I was familiar with until my late forties. Taking a pivot in my faith journey, separate from the check boxes, was and is not encouraged. Honestly, I didn't realize it was an option.

Differentiation may take us in unexpected, new, and different places; by "different," I mean not the prescribed "norm." When this happens, some experiencing differentiation are told, "No, that's wrong" and are even shamed, judged, or ostracized for following the natural course (natural for them and their experience) of learning and growth. Then, as they follow their natural course and stop "checking all the boxes," these individuals internalize that shame, judgment, and ostracization that has been heaped on them from others.

---

[1] https://dictionary.cambridge.org
[2] https://www.thebowencenter.org/differentiation-of-self

Interfering with the natural course of things weakens communities. If we ignore, discourage, or try to stop differentiation of one's faith development, we miss the bigger picture. We miss the whole point of growing faith organically when we try to grow it by force, certainty, or using just one set, prescribed path.

We miss the beauty that is there to observe, and the lessons to be had and discovered that will deepen and cement faith in ways not otherwise possible. We miss growth that comes from sources not yet known to us because we don't even give ourselves permission to seek such sources, let alone trust the journey of seeking.

Not only does certainty weaken communities, it stymies the individual. Certainty is a lie that when believed keeps us from seeking, questioning, and basking in the glory of curiosity.

Interestingly enough, "certainty" can't even be certain. Not even science can lean into and claim absolute certainty. Anyone fighting cancer knows "NED" is not "certainty." *No Evidence of Disease* (NED) is not the same as *cancer free*. It's not the same as saying *with certainty* that treatments for cancer are complete and done forever.

So, if and when you start to feel like you're standing out from those around you, or that your pathway, your journey is looking different from those around you, this is your reminder that it's **supposed to be that way.**

Notice your perception of self. If you define yourself using external sources—the expectations other people have of you, the accomplishments you do or do not achieve related to said expectations, and subsequent attention, accolades, or recognition you may or may not receive for those accomplishments—you are basing your definition of self on things *outside of your control.* Therefore, your sense of self is outside of you. The reverse is also true. Adjusting your focus to that which is *inside* of you, within your control, creates a sense of self that is grounded and centered in who you actually are, have been, and are becoming.

Finding your internal definition of self requires more effort, searching, trusting, believing. This demands that you ignore the chatter outside of you and learn to quiet yourself enough to "hear" the whispers of your inner self—your soul.

This also means you choose to show up regardless of how others show up. You intentionally choose to define yourself and how you will be, what you will say, what you will do, and so on in any given situation no matter what others do and say or don't do and say. Period. This isn't easy, and it takes practice.

On my podcast, *Beyond the Shadow of Doubt*™, I've had the privilege of interviewing folks who have decided to show up intentionally. They are choosing to lean into discomfort in the most profound ways and decide on purpose what they will say and do, and not say and not do, and not just as guests I interviewed for the podcast. They are seekers, believers, doubters, persons of faith, questioners, and leaders of themselves. They are learning to claim self-sovereignty.

In their faith and in their journey, each one of these beautiful souls has claimed their sovereignty for themselves, and let me tell you—it is breathtaking. This could only come about through differentiation.

This is the true way of shining our unique light.

In nature, it's a completely normal phenomenon to see differentiation—found in a variety of forms—that comes with growth and maturation.

For instance, with cancer, the term "cell differentiation" is defined by The National Cancer Institute as, "The process during which young, immature (unspecialized) cells take on individual characteristics and reach their mature (specialized) form and function."[3]

In plant and animal development, as cells divide, grow, and amass they eventually make up lifegiving tissues, organs, and organ systems like root systems[4].

Each individual cell is important and holds a vital role. This is your reminder that in all of nature, differentiation is requisite and contributes to the health and functioning of the organism as a whole.

It is the natural differentiation of cells as they mature that makes it possible to target the cancerous ones and try to save as many of the good cells as possible.

In many ways, religion is like a living organism. Mormonism is a religion that has been going through the dividing and expanding process over the past 200+ years. It does have a variety of cells; however, I'm not sure differentiation has actually occurred when the individual cells (members) within have attempted it. Mormonism is my cultural heritage. It is part of my human experience and has shaped so much of who I am. It is part of my DNA.

Regardless of your faith background, I invite you to take inventory of the ways in which you engage in discussion, be it with loved ones, neighbors, or folks in and outside of your faith community. No matter where *they* are on *their* faith journey-crisis-expansion, ASK yourself, "How can I keep emotions in check when discussing things we may not agree on, and focus on making sure this individual feels SEEN and HEARD?"

That's it. I really believe this is the only way to get some open, genuine, respectful, loving conversations started. There are so

---

[3]https://www.cancer.gov/publications/dictionaries/cancer-terms/def/cell-differentiation
[4]https://organismalbio.biosci.gatech.edu/growth-and-reproduction/plant-development-i-tissue-differentiation-and-function

many areas where this is applicable, not just in faith communities but also in relationships, families, politics, and corporate settings.

Can you differentiate yourself enough to honor your beliefs *and* your neighbor's? And can you go a step further and show your respect for your neighbors' beliefs, modeling for them the way to establish mutual respect between you and at least attempt to live in some type of harmony?

I propose we can, and I will, and I did. I will share two experiences with you.

In September of 2024, I attended the Gather Conference in Provo, Utah. While in Utah, I made sure to visit the acclaimed Compass Gallery, which at the time had the *First Be Reconciled* exhibit, which, according to their website was:

> *An immersive exhibition of painting and sculpture exploring apologies and reconciliation in religious community, by J. Kirk Richards.*
>
> *Of worship and repentance, Jesus said, "First be reconciled to your brother or sister, and then come and offer your gift." Apologies are powerful. In the absence of an institutional apology, there may yet be power in the apologies of its members. Please feel encouraged to write your own respectful apologies on behalf of our community and add them to mine. My apologies are written on yellow paper. Inside, you'll find QR codes and links to related organizations you can donate to, should you feel so inclined, to take our apology a step further.*

Apologies are indeed powerful, as I learned when I wrote my own. I knelt at the altar under the painting, "We Have Set Our Rainbow in the Clouds," which depicts two heavenly beings lovingly creating a beautiful rainbow in the clouds. I could not hold back the tears rolling down my cheeks as I wrote:

September 13, 2024

To my beloved queer siblings, friends, family members:

I am sorry it took me so long to "see" you.

I am sorry you are not seen, still, by so many.

The tides are changing.

And like the moon, I am using my energy to pull that tide with _all my might_!

I love you.

Thank you for teaching me.

Meagan Renee' Schultz Skidmore

Picture of me writing this letter at the Compass Gallery Exhibit:

After I wrote this, I rolled it up into a nice little scroll, tied it with a string, and tucked it in with the rest of the apologies written by other patrons. Richards knew what he was doing with this collection. There were other paintings reflecting the possibility for collective and individual apologies for wrongs to other marginalized folks, including women and people of color.

It was potent and so very powerful to write from my heart. Even though it wasn't addressed to any one person specifically, I was surprised at how I struggled to write. I wanted so badly to find the right words. I was careful in choosing my words to express what surfaced at that moment from my heart.

In May of 2022, President Russell M. Nelson gave a message to a group of young adults. In this address he shared the following:

> "Any *abuse* or *prejudice* towards another because of nationality, race, sexual orientation, gender, educational degrees, culture, or other significant identifiers is offensive to our Maker! Such mistreatment causes us to live beneath our stature as His covenant sons and daughters."[5]

In my observation, this statement *does* contradict what has recently been included, or updated, in the LDS Church's Handbook. (You can read the updates here—scan the QR code below—or go to the website [see footnote[6]].)

---

[5] "The Prophet Says Now Is When We Choose How We Will Live Forever," 15 May 2022, Salt Lake City, UT, The Church of Jesus Christ of Latter-day Saints

[6] https://assets.churchofjesuschrist.org/1d/76/1d76991533df11efbaeeeeeeac1ed7e66 fbf94a7/general_handbook_guiding_principles_for_local_leaders.pdf.

PDF of August
2024 LDS policy

To release policies, rules, tenets (what you call them matters much less than the outcome they produce) that address what transgender and nonbinary individuals are allowed and not allowed to do or what they are qualified to participate in automatically calls into question their legitimacy, validity, and humanness.

The implicit message perpetuates and deepens bias, bigotry, fear, and exclusion already in existence, and the explicit outcome is often worse: it gives an out to those unwilling to address their own personal discomfort with the issue. They feel justified in words and behaviors that most would classify as "unChristlike" because "that is what the handbook says." It does not encourage thinking for oneself, or in other words—differentiation.

When words of this nature are published by a respected and revered institution, members take those words to be doctrine and then absorb and follow the message. I address this because unless you *purposely choose proximity*, there are stories about which you may be unaware. These are stories of mistreatment and unmerited discipline, like actions toward transgender and nonbinary persons. And unfortunately, even more tragically, some who identify as transgender and nonbinary unalive themselves because the fear and hate is too great for them to bear.

It is for this reason I chose to address my concerns in the following letter that I sent to lgbt@churchofjesuschrist.org shortly after the handbook changes that targeted transgender and nonbinary individuals:

Dear Sirs:

I write to express deep concern about the recent changes in the General Handbook regarding Individuals Who Identify as Transgender (Section 38.6.23) and the accompanying guiding principles.

I have asked myself, "Where is the love" in these changes, and I have to be honest, I do not feel nor see it.

I do not see how these policies reflect the love Jesus Christ has for these individuals or His teachings about the commandment to love one another. They do not align with the Lord and Savior I have come to know whose entire ministry was focused on reaching out to, loving, and including those who are marginalized. That's what made him so radical in a time when many in society distanced themselves from those "less than," beneath, or different than themselves.

I believe these policies do not reflect the values of my Savior. They have no place in a church that has Jesus Christ at its head. As long as they are in place, transgender and nonbinary individuals will receive the message that the God who supposedly created them is not okay with them and sees them as mistakes to be "fixed" or "tolerated." I humbly request that those with authority review and revise these policies to reflect the example and teachings of our Savior, and to do so immediately. Policies such as these send a message that it were better to unalive oneself than live as their true authentic self as a transgender or nonbinary individual.

These policies reflect current societal prejudice and fear rather than what is needed and deserved by those who are transgender. They perpetuate said prejudice and fear and provide a source for those unwilling to step outside of discomfort to confirm their biases rather than challenge them. This makes policies such as these deeply, profoundly harmful and unworthy of the Church of Jesus Christ.

As a parent of a beautiful, steadfast, transgender son, I am intimately aware of the harm Church policy can cause. The pain of exclusion and the cognitive dissonance caused by the messages of being deemed a sin/sinful for merely the way they were born, caused serious mental health challenges and led to him no longer feeling safe in the only church (and ward) he had ever known. As a mother, it has been excruciating to witness my child question that God loves them, or else why would they be viewed in this way by the church whose leaders professes to speak for God. It sends a tragically mixed, harmful message.

The loss of his spiritual home has been devastating for our family, immediate and extended. Some family members have also followed suit. As a 6th generation member of the Church, having been raised LDS, to have cherished family members feel and be excluded has been an immense loss.

Our pain is shared by many, many transgender individuals and their families and loved ones.

We are deeply troubled that the General Handbook changes of August 2024 reinforce attitudes of prejudice and fear by treating transgender individuals as physically and morally dangerous. Judgment of a person based on the expression of their [gender] identity is discrimination and is not in harmony with the gospel of Jesus Christ.

Our Savior showed that to love and heal we must transcend cultural and religious barriers and embrace those who are feared, judged, and excluded. If a member is uncomfortable about the inclusion of a transgender person, leaders could encourage them to do as Christ did in His ministry and get closer, reach out to the outcasts and the marginalized. Love them, listen to them, see them. Leaders can show the way by getting to know the trans member and/or their family personally.

We believe that all members of the Church are harmed by policies of exclusion and discrimination, because each member, with their diverse identities, experiences, and perspectives is needed, and we must learn to love and care for one another to build Zion. Any message that one is not allowed or doesn't fit sends a message that anyone who is different does not belong, is not welcome.

The Church's stance on gender identity does not reconcile with my (our) lived experiences or those of the transgender individuals I know personally. Sacred experiences have reinforced to me our collective responsibility to love, accept, support, and walk beside those in the transgender community.

My testimony of Christ's love and our capacity to feel and express God's love have been magnified many times over by my close association with transgender loved ones. I am profoundly saddened that the Church continues to make and expand policies that harm these precious, vulnerable individuals and the membership as a whole.

Again, I humbly request that those with authority to do so immediately review and revise these policies to reflect the example and teachings of our Savior and send the message that all belong and are welcome.

Sincerely,

Meagan Skidmore, M.S., School Counseling Psychologist, Life Transitions Coach

In full disclosure, my dear friend Dr. Julia Campbell Bernards wrote a stirring letter, and it is from those inspired words I created mine. It is with her permission that I share her letter sent to the same email address.

Dear Sirs:

We are writing to express our deep concern about the recent changes in the General Handbook regarding Individuals Who Identify as Transgender (Section 38.6.23) and the guiding principles which accompany it.

We believe these policies are not reflective of Christ's love for these individuals or of His teachings about how we must love one another. We believe these policies have no place in a church that has Jesus Christ at its head. We humbly request that those with authority to do so immediately

review and revise these policies to reflect the example and teachings of our Savior.

We believe these policies reflect current societal prejudice and fear rather than the will of the Lord or what is needed and deserved by those who are transgender. We see these policies as deeply harmful and unworthy of the Church of Jesus Christ.

As parents of a beautiful, steadfast, transgender daughter, we are intimately aware of the harm Church policy can cause. The policies about transgender individuals that went into effect in January 2020 excluded our worthy daughter from cherished temple attendance and a joyfully anticipated full-time mission. The pain of exclusion and the cognitive dissonance caused by the difference between her lived experiences and personal revelation and the Church's teachings caused serious mental health challenges and led to her no longer feeling safe in the only church she had ever known. Her loss of her spiritual home was devastating for our whole family.

Our pain is shared by many, many transgender individuals and their families and loved ones.

We are deeply troubled that the General Handbook changes of August 2024 reinforce attitudes of prejudice and fear by treating transgender individuals as physically and morally dangerous. Judgment of a person based on the expression of their [gender] identity is discrimination and is not in harmony with the gospel of Jesus Christ.

Our Savior showed that to love and heal we must transcend cultural and religious barriers and embrace those who are feared, judged, and excluded. If a member is uncomfortable about the inclusion of a transgender person, leaders could encourage them to meditate on Christ's ministry and invite them to get to know the trans member and/or their family personally.

We believe that all members of the Church are harmed by policies of exclusion and discrimination, because each member, with their diverse identities, experiences, and perspectives is needed and we must learn to love and care for one another to build Zion.

The Church's stance on gender identity does not reconcile with our lived experiences or those of the transgender individuals we know personally. We have had sacred experiences that reinforce our responsibility to love, accept, support, and walk beside those in the transgender community.

Our testimony of Christ's love and our capacity to feel and express God's love have been magnified by our close association with transgender loved ones. We are profoundly saddened that the Church continues to make and expand policies that harm these precious, vulnerable individuals and the membership as a whole.

Again, we humbly request that those with authority to do so immediately review and revise these policies to reflect the example and teachings of our Savior.

Sincerely,
Dr. Julia Campbell Bernards

So, which is the inspired one: the 2022 message from President Russell M. Nelson, or the August 2024 LDS Handbook updates?

This is a rhetorical question and one I do not intend to answer.

As I have claimed my spiritual sovereignty, I reject anything that conflicts with who I know God to be. I will not internalize anything that contradicts, compromises, or questions my inherent worth, or that of my friends and loved ones. Period.

Civil Rights activist Ella Baker said, "Give people light and they will find a way."[7]

Here's the thing I believe about light: it is, at present, within you. It IS the Divinity *already* within you. Before we can "give light" or shine our unique light, it is requisite to connect with and see it for ourselves within our own Divine beings.

The lighthouse does not scamper about, up and down the sand and rocks in an effort to get the attention of the vessels upon the sea and share its bright light. No, instead, it remains firmly upon the solid foundation of the shore, beckoning weary travelers to safety, if they resonate with and follow the beaming light.

This is translucence.

---

[7] Quoted in *I've Got the Light of Freedom: The Organizing Tradition and The Mississippi Freedom Struggle* by Charles M. Payne.

4

TRANSITION

(the act of passing from one state or place to the next; another name for sunrise and sunset)

It doesn't matter how the child you're loving came into your life and your heart, everyone raising a child is intimately familiar with the pain and beauty of contractions—the rhythm of "holding on tight" and "letting go." From wobbly first steps to college drop-offs, embrace-release is a form of love that can leave stretch marks on our hearts. If you're knee-deep in bittersweet this season, you're not alone.

~ Brené Brown (via email newsletter)

All my life
I've been sittin' at the table
Watchin' them kids, they're living in a fable
Looks, luck, money and never left a'wishin'
But now it's 'bout time to raise up and petition

———

'Cause I've been wondering
When you gonna see I'm not for sale
I've been questioning
When you gonna see I'm not a part of your machine
Not a part of your machine

I'm not scared of what you're gonna tell me
No, I'm not scared of the beast in the belly
Fill my cup with endless ambition
And paint this town with my very own vision

———

'Cause I've been wondering
When you gonna see I'm not for sale
I've been questioning
When you gonna see I'm not a part of your machine
Not a part of your machine

I am the machine

> ~ "Machine," recorded by Imagine Dragons, written by Alexander Junior Grant, Benjamin Arthur Mckee, Daniel Coulter Reynolds, Daniel James Platzman, and Daniel Wayne Sermon.

*Some names in this chapter have been changed to protect privacy

December 4, 2023

I hurt. I hurt emotionally so badly right now and have for several days. Where is all this pain coming from? It has been building up since about two Sundays ago. I can't afford to have this keep happening. It is so painful to be at church on Sundays . . . so painful . . . This last time I attended sent me in a tailspin.

I'm stuck. I've been lethargic for days. I have so much shame around that too.

Why can't I lean into what my intuition seems to be telling me??? Do I even know? Can I access it???? Ugh.

Faith journeys/expansions/crises SUCK. Sometimes I wish I had never been born in this church. Sometimes, I feel like the first 50 years of my life I've been short-changed. Other times, I'm grateful for my spirituality, I just have a hard time separating it from the crap that religion brings with it.

Waking up is HARD as hell.

Having a spiritual awakening has been the most painful thing I've experienced so far. I have so much anger lately; it shows up as shutting down. I'm so stuck, so stuck. I hate that this is my journey. I hate it. I didn't choose this; it truly feels like it chose me.

Idk.

I'm so angry. Angry enough to scream . . . and yet, I have no energy to mutter a peep, let alone scream. And to add insult to injury, I'm beating myself up inside. using the progress (or "lack of") in my biz against myself.

Ugh.

I just want the world to stop. I need a break. I need a safe place. I don't have a safe place, at least it doesn't seem like it. I can only "dump" so much on others . . . and the deeper into this journey I go, the less I'm able to trust folks that I have been able to trust so far.

> It feels like they can't understand me . . . because my experience is so very different.
>
> Why do I care if they judge me? Idk.
>
> Why do I care so much about what others may or may not think??
>
> Who the hell cares??? Why do I care so much?
>
> Idk. Idk.
>
> I'm so sad. So lost. So depressed. I barely want to get out of bed. I'm so overwhelmed.

I wasn't sure whether to include this journal entry or not. It's pretty raw. I decided to share it because, although I couldn't see or know it at the time, I know now that I was experiencing the deep visceral mental, emotional, spiritual, and physical pain of transition. This is an essential part of the journey of transformation, and then, eventual transcendence. Until I re-read it and decided to include it, I had forgotten how much pain I was in and how angry I was.

I was so angry.

I share this with you to offer you an olive branch of hope. It does get better.

Whatever you are feeling now IS NOT YOU.

It doesn't define you nor have to limit you. It is temporary. The greatest gift you can give yourself is to allow it, feel it, and get yourself the support you need.

It's easy to forget that feelings and thoughts aren't facts. They aid us as we navigate life's vast array of experiences. They play the part of supporting roles in the stories we create in our efforts to make sense of our world.

If feelings and thoughts are supporting actors in our stories, decisions are the leading role. Decisions aren't a friend or a foe. They offer needed insight that comes from the *process* of making a choice and then *witnessing the outcome* of that choice. They are a tool that helps guide us along as we choose one turn or fork in the road over another. Some turns we find out are meant for us, others are under construction, and still others are detours where we learn hard lessons.

That is all they are; they are neutral. Humans can get into trouble when they attach meaning to their thoughts, feelings, or decisions. Attaching meaning isn't a problem, per se, unless it is not serving us and is causing us harm.

Writing or journaling is a key that unlocks the door to receiving deeper insight into what our stories are and the meaning we are making about them.

December 7, 2023

Writing workshop number two. Free flow writing.

I have been overcome by fear. Triggers?

I have mentally/emotionally taken a turn since two Sundays ago. Going to church on Sundays takes a toll on my mental health. It's really hard to be there and not be triggered. And yet, I continue to go. Sigh.

Maybe it was the episode where I was recently interviewed by "Papa" Richard Ostler on the *Listen, Learn, and Love* podcast and shared my story.

Or maybe it was going to church two Sundays ago and crying on Carol's shoulder. At the close of the meeting, while singing the closing hymn, I was overcome with emotion as I tried to sing the words. They wouldn't come; I couldn't choke them out.

Or perhaps it was being confused by Wanda coming up to me after the closing prayer and hugging me. She actually said, "I love you." That has never happened before. Was it sincere? What was it? I wasn't sure what to think.

Over the next few days, I slowly went down emotionally.

Why am I triggered by this stuff?

Do I not believe that they are acting sincerely?

Why have I gotten to this place of fear the past two weeks?

I guess when I'm flooded, I'm really flooded, and I have no choice but to honor that, allow it, and feel it. I know old patterns of thoughts kick in. Many of them center around shame, very self-deprecating thoughts.

That's not good, is it? Why do I only see negative? I know there are positives. I worry that my mental health struggles are inherited, and I'll never escape them.

I got on a Zoom call this morning to help fellow coach Joy out by being a participant for a practice run of a speech. Another fellow coach who was a participant on the call greeted me and said, "Hello!" and "You're one of my favorite people."

What? Why do I struggle to believe that?

Why do I judge myself so harshly?

I noticed that a recent podcast guest reposted and shared our podcast interview to a private parent group. She started out by saying, "I was recently interviewed by our amazing Meagan Skidmore . . ."

Why did that make my heart jump? Why is my knee-jerk reaction to care what was said, define myself by it . . . and then trickle to a place of self-doubt or telling myself that "they are just saying that"?

The admin of the group, Harriet, commented on it and said, "Just listened. Highly recommend."

I commented, "Thank you; one day I would love to have you on the podcast."

Why did my thoughts go to, "I don't want her to feel bad," or "would she even want to be on my podcast?"

I noticed Kelly, another parent I'd already interviewed on my podcast, put hearts in a comment on this same post. I replied, "I loved having you as a guest; thank you for sharing your heart."

I can see I went there because I'm projecting on them, possibly what I might feel if the table was turned. I'd want to be acknowledged. Why do I still care about external validation?

I've noticed that I really feel strongly about having ALL voices on my podcast, not limiting it to "one type of believer" or another. No way. Not at all.

Harriet is out of the LDS faith. To me, her story is still so super valid and important. In some ways, I envy her; she's made her choice and seemingly moved on and is happy. I don't know that for sure; I'm projecting on her, I guess.

But being willing to have all voices on my podcast . . . I think this is my way of dissolving the "Us vs. Them" line in the sand. Actually, a lot of the time it feels like it's drawn in concrete and solidified.

And ISN'T it all a SPECTRUM anyway?

Belief is a spectrum!

Why must we choose some random, proverbial place on that line of how far "in or out" we are in our faith practices, beliefs, and understandings? Won't mine be different from my neighbor's? Yes.

How do I know that my neighbor is defining it in the same way as I am? I don't. That's the thing.

Can I even compare my understanding with another? Not really. I'm not a mind reader.

AND

Why does it even matter?

Why must we judge or try to determine at which point a person is on their proverbial x and y axis that supposedly represents something as deep and personal and sacred as their relationship with the Divine?

As I type this (or say it out loud) it doesn't even make sense. It sounds preposterous.

I don't want to have to choose to be all in or all out, nor do I want anyone else to have to do so either, unless they want to and it feels 100% aligned for them to do so—that's totally different.

To choose using free will to be one or the other, that's one's right to do so. But what if I don't like those options? What if one day I want to attend church and others I don't even want to talk about it because of the hurt I am processing, caused by words, actions, policies, and doctrines of the church?

Can we just normalize that WE ARE NOT BINARY like computer programming code? We are not either a zero or a one.

WE ARE BOTH AND *everything* in *between,* and *before,* and *beyond.*

WE ARE FOUR D (4-D) beings living in a 2-D realm.

I am processing so fucking much hurt.

I HURT. BAD.

SO. BAD.

I don't say the F-word, except maybe 5 times in my life. Now 6 times. (I'm kidding. I haven't kept track).

I have never experienced something so isolating, emotionally depriving, soul-vacating, and harrowing. I simultaneously feel like I exist and that I don't exist.

If there is a hell, I. Am. Here.

I have **no** fear of it in the afterlife. I am experiencing it **now**.

There is this horizontal pull I feel from my crown to my heels. This polarity is ripping through my soul in ways for which I do not have words.

Choose between God or your child.

Rip. Slash. Tear. Pull.

Choose between the faith of your heritage or your family.

Tug. Tear. Sear. Pull.

Choose between believing your worth as a being of Divine origin or your value plummets to absolute zero.

Sear. Pull. Slash. Shred.

How am I still walking, standing, feeling, breathing . . . alive?

This experience is soul, bone, spirit crushing.

Years ago, while walking to elementary school alone, I came face-to-face with a VERY large dog that wasn't on a leash. I'm not 100% sure, but I think it was a German Shephard. All I remember is that it was BIG and LOUD. It was almost as tall as me, or so it seemed, and its incessant barking hurt my ears and pierced my heart, and not in a good way.

I was terrified.

He was outside, unattended, in front of the house. In an eyeblink, he was across the carport and had stopped directly in front of me, barking madly the entire time. He had positioned himself squarely on the secret sidewalk between me and the way to school. The barking would not stop, nor was I allowed to pass by.

I was absolutely petrified.

As I was trembling, I remembered something my mom taught me, and that was to plant my feet firmly, not move, and shake my finger sternly while yelling, "STAY!" I did that more times than I can remember. It didn't change the dog's mind a single bit, but it did alert the owner, who eventually came out (after 1 million years) and yelled at the dog to stop and come in.

I can still remember the relief I felt while simultaneously feeling anger at the owner for having been so careless.

This is not an isolated incident from my past, and most likely, you have one similar that you can recall. Collectively, it is these traumatic experiences that can hinder us from "transitioning" or "transitions."

These traumatic experiences are like the scratches, dents, dings, and warping that collect on a vinyl record over the course of time. During the Advanced Relationship Trauma Certification I completed with Lindsay Poelman, she taught,

> *This is a way to think about the nervous system. Generally speaking, we come to Earth and—if you think about coming to Earth like a vinyl record— when our vinyl record is printed, it's clean. There aren't any skips or divots when you buy it fresh off the press. As circumstances arise in life, you might get little scratches and divots. . . .*

She further explained that our vinyl record is like a blueprint, or our "true self." It is childhood experiences—like getting lost at Disneyland or almost getting attacked by a giant dog while walking to elementary school—that leave a mark. Even though we are eventually found at Disneyland or make it through the almost dog attack physically unscathed, there is great potential for these experiences to create (or imprint) skips, scratches, and divots upon our vinyl record, blueprint, or true self.

Until we are able to get the needed, appropriate mental health support to address the trauma, our vinyl record will remind us and elicit a similar response each time it passes over the skips, scratches, and divots.

It took a long time for me to get over my fear of dogs, both from that experience and another when my brother was attacked while riding a bike. And I won't give details, but I will share that to this day, I have experiences where my responses remind me (carry the residue?) of the lasting effects of the sexual abuse I experienced in childhood.

In September 2024, on a hot yet beautiful day at Cedar Ridge Preserve, I went for a solo hike, and my head was abuzz with so much chatter that I decided to record it. I wrote:

> I'm noticing no matter who I pass, I'm suspicious of; I can see my issues of trust bubbling up simply being out here on this hike. I'm by myself, and I think the only time I didn't come up with a reason that somebody could potentially be dangerous is if they were also a woman out here alone, or once, when I was walking by a little family—two parents, male and female, and their almost 4-year-old child. I know because I chatted with them.
>
> Even when a guy walked by coming from the opposite direction, with a big ole cross necklace, my thought at first was, "He's a Christian; he's not a threat," and less than a split second later my next thought was, "That could just be a front to pretend he is something he's not."
>
> A couple times when I found myself passing by a heterosexual couple (at least they were seemingly heterosexual), my thought was, "Maybe they are a pair, and she's just complacent or powerless. Perhaps their

hetero-facing relationship is a ploy to lure unsuspecting victims in."

Another time I passed a single male coming from the opposite direction, who, for all intents and purposes, was bigger than me, had more muscles than me, and was big and smiley. I made a point to make eye contact and say hello or good day or good afternoon. It seemed friendly enough, but then as soon as we passed, in a split second, I caught a huge whiff of his cologne. Suspicion immediately settled in. "Oh," I thought, "his ploy is to lure them in with scents and smiles and friendliness."

Is this just because I'm alone, or do I do this if I'm with a friend as well?! I don't know for sure, but I don't think so. I think it is mostly when I'm alone. My awareness is heightened, and I am vigilant about watching my surroundings.

The effects of trauma are exhausting.

What I wrote represents my mind chatter more than I realized. My awareness has been elevated this past year because I am writing a book. I don't typically record my thoughts to this extent.

But it did provide me with insight. In anything in life, there really is no point of arrival. There is always more to see, experience, learn, and grow from. It is cyclical, not linear, so even when you know or see something, the next time around there will be a new, deeper, more insightful layer.

Not just during this hike, but certainly through it, I was reminded just how lifelong and deeply embedded my issues with trust have been: SOOOO deep. I realized I struggle to this day with trust and shame, and it's possible I always will to some degree.

Each time I acknowledge them, face them, and deal with them, my stories surrounding shame and trust loosen their grip and dissolve a little more. There is an embrace-release rhythm to this process, like contractions, that leave stretch marks as I heal.

During this hike, I really became aware of my inner child bubbling up, popping her head in, trying to keep me safe. I noted how I have come to thank her for watching out for me and assure her that I am indeed safe.

Will I ever be able to believe I am completely safe? I don't have the answer. But I will and do have the tools to remind younger me that I am safe *now*, in the present moment. I've learned to transition stories, or *the act of passing from one state or place to the next*.

I literally offer calm, logical, clear words of comfort as I guide little me. I remind her that the resourced, adult version of me knows how to move from that place, or story, that creates distrust or shame and transition it to one of love, confidence, belief, and knowing. It is a mind transition, an exercise in metacognition.

Life is a series of one transition after another. In the Fall of 2023, I had the privilege of interviewing Bree Borrowman, a beautiful transgender woman. Her wise words have stayed with me ever since.

> *It's not just one event. It's a journey. For me, and I think for most people . . . transitioning is not a one-day thing.*

> *It's not like, "Oh, this happened. OK, I'm gonna be my authentic self." And so it is a process that you go through.*

> *I had some friends who introduced me to a friend of theirs, a new acquaintance. They said to me, "So, Bree! Tell us. When was it? Or how long? Or how? When did you? When did you transition?"*

And I said, "Well, when did you?"

Then they're like, "What?!"

*And I said, **"We're all in a state of transitioning**. Everybody is different today than they were ten years ago. You're different than you were when you were a teenager. You're different than when you were twenty-five. Everybody transitions in their life. Life in itself is a journey of transitioning from one type of individual to [another] . . . I mean, we **all** change all the time."*[8]

I see transition in so many places now. I see it in the sunrises and sunsets. At what point does the sunset end and dusk begin?

That begs the question, at what point has dusk come to a close, and the blanket of night settles on the land, the trees, the animals, the humans, the hearts, the minds, the souls?

Is it with the presence of the stars and the moon?

That can't be it because they are always there regardless of whether the naked human eye can see them or not.

At what point does the blanket of night start to pull back its corners and roll away from its comfortable position of snuggling into the earth and allow dawn to start to make its entrance?

When does dawn eventually give way to the rays of sun coming from Father Sky to light up Mother Earth, alerting all that another new day on this planet is coming and offering welcome and greetings?

Maybe there's not supposed to be a beginning or an end.

Maybe that's the point. Maybe it's all just one great, big middle that we are each experiencing in different ways because our literal

---

[8] *Living Beyond the Shadow of Doubt* podcast, Episodes 89 and 90, "I Am Finally Me with Bree Borrowman, Parts 1 and 2."

viewpoints—the point at which we stand to view this grand artwork of Mother Nature—are all different!

And maybe that's also the point!

What resonates or is beautiful to me is simply OK for someone else as they get it from their viewpoint. Or they see something else as grand and majestic that I find just OK.

For instance, someone who only knows the rotation of the earth axis from the latitude of Iceland might find the experience in the Caribbean beautiful and amazing and warm and welcoming and bright and light and all of those things. And I, who was born in Arizona and knows the rays of the sun oh-so very well, might find it just another degree of Dante's Inferno. I may not experience it in the same way that the Icelander does.

A Sherpa born and raised on Mount Kilimanjaro could find a backpacking trip into the depths of the Grand Canyon fascinating and awe inspiring, or they could be like, "Meh, I've seen much bigger than this," lol.

Not all trees point upward. The weeping willow or weeping pine tree (I don't know the name of it) bends its long, trailing gown toward Mother Earth.

The thing about being out in nature is we each get the lessons and the messages custom made for us. There's a lot going on, but different folks here will pick up on different things. Someone will notice the shadows of the trees creating movement on the ground. Someone else might notice as the wind shakes the leaves on the oaks and the evergreens. And still another will notice the feeling of the wind gently caressing and embracing their sweaty skin.

Some will notice the babbling of the birds in the trees, and others, like me for a while, will be so focused on all of the dead leaves on the ground, vigilantly watching for any of the native snakes to make an unwelcome appearance.

And still, others will be watching for the next nearest bench or stump to sit down on, and rest their bones, and catch their breath.

While hiking at Cedar Ridge Preserve, I did notice while in those moments of pause, sitting on the naturemade benches to catch my breath, that when others walked by, *I surrendered.* I was so physically exhausted that I knew if danger did present itself, I would have no recourse. I was too tired and had absolutely no energy to fight. So, I had no choice but to release, allow, and surrender to my fears of, "What if?"

When two male hikers walked by, and I was still sitting and out of breath, my thoughts went, *Oh well, I can't move. I will just have to trust . . . trust myself, trust them, trust the circumstances, trust my know-how, trust my instincts and my abilities.*

Interesting how much quicker my thoughts will reflect confidence or demonstrate resilience in the face of *whatever comes up* (uncertainty), and how deeper and more intensely I feel both resilience and confidence. This confidence I feel doesn't just bubble up to the surface; it's front and center.

When I told myself, *I will just have to trust . . .* I meant it. I can feel it to my bones. At this moment, there is no mistaking it. I feel this way again.

I completed the loop along the pond of Cattail Trail at Cedar Ridge Preserve. Each time I came to a crossroads, there were various outlets to choose from. I picked the one that, according to my Strava map, seemed like the one that would get me back to my original starting point. Never having been here before, I saw that this resulted in making a giant loop.

The symbolism is not lost on me.

Isn't that what we all do? Whenever we're at a crossroads in life, we check our guide posts—left by ones who came before us— we make the best judgment call from that map, and then we trust. We don't know how it will turn out until it turns out.

To hike the crossroads of life, we each prepare for the journey in different ways.

On this trail at Cedar Ridge Preserve, I noticed some wore tanks, shorts, and appropriate socks and tennis shoes or hiking shoes. I saw one woman in a tennis skirt and tech shirt. Some were in casual T-shirts and cargo shorts, and others wore long, jogging pants suits with a jacket covering the T-shirt underneath. Another adventurous hiker was taking a jog in long jeans, flat tennis shoes, and a T-shirt. I saw someone in a lovely wide-rimmed, straw hat and sunglasses. Most had some type of earbuds or AirPods in their ears.

Did I mention it was 90° outside in the shade? Some had zero water bottles (or any bottle with some kind of fluid to drink). Some had backpacks containing water bottles and snacks. Others had backpacks carrying a large speaker blaring their favorite music. Still others were dressed in street clothes and tennis shoes resembling kids from the '80s while carrying their purses as though they were out for a stroll.

One unsuspecting dad struggled to push his toddler in a stroller over some very rocky, bumpy, uneven terrain. This vehicle, or stroller, was not created to navigate said terrain.

And believe it or not, I saw a guy jogging in flip-flops.

Does that mean some were right and some wrong? Or that some were prepared and others weren't, and they would all get what they deserve? No, I don't believe that to be true.

Maybe they just didn't have the guidance, tutelage, insight, or exposure beforehand to have an idea of what to expect, what to bring, or what to wear. It is easy to forget there is privilege in that. I choose to believe they were doing the best they could with what they had by way of resources, information, talents, and abilities.

I didn't expect it, but during this hike, my inner child—the one who didn't feel safe, protected, or able to trust—came up screaming.

Even with mental health support like therapy, trauma work, and even coaching, those skips, divots, and scratches are not completely buffed out. They most likely never will be.

That is OK. It makes a world of difference having the tools to calm our inner child, to navigate what remains of the buffed scratches, detecting them in advance, seeing the warning signs up ahead, and also knowing what to do to create safety for ourselves as we pass through, over, or by them.

This is transition.

**Scan this QR Code for tools to help you calm your inner child:

"10 Tools and Practices to Calm Your Inner Child'"

use code TRANSPARENTSEE

TransparentSEE

5

TRANSIENCE
(constantly changing)

Five years and there's no doubt
That I'm burned out, I've had enough

———

Some believe in destiny and some believe in fate
But I believe that happiness is something we create
You best believe that I'm not gonna wait
'Cause there's gotta be somethin' more

———

I need a little less hard time, I need a little more bliss
I'm gonna take my chances
Takin' a chance I might
Find what I've been lookin' for
Gotta be somethin' more

~ "Something More," recorded by Sugarland, written by
Jennifer Nettles, Kristian Bush, and Kristen Hall

The Russians are coming.

I grew up with a literal fear of "the Russians." The cold war was real. I was genuinely fearful of an impending threat of nuclear war. In my underdeveloped mind, and with minimal knowledge, understanding, and experience I had concluded Russians must be pretty scary folks. They were the enemy. This may sound a bit far-fetched, but this was the reality of the 1980s, when I was young and in grade school. All I knew was what family members, neighbors, teachers, news reporters, and other adults around me were saying about Russia.

It wasn't until 2010, when I had the opportunity to visit Moscow and St. Petersburg, that I got to see and experience the Russian people for myself. I realized that they were just people, exactly like me, each with ten fingers and ten toes. They weren't scary. One-on-one, up close and personal, it was obvious that they experienced much of life like I did— faith, families, friends, relationships, being out in the plazas or markets, enjoying meals and quality time with one another. The food they ate was different, and their homes looked different, but the commonalities outweighed the differences.

After believing a certain way for almost forty years, I did, in fact, change my mind. I realized how wrongly they had been portrayed by the media. In the process of changing my mind, I released the fear my inner child had so many years ago that "the Russians are coming." My visit to Russia and assimilation of new information dissolved the lingering fear I felt surrounding the stories I held from childhood as a result of growing up in the era of the cold war.

Can you change your mind?

Recently in my work, a client with evolving beliefs shared that a loved one, in a straightforward manner, said, "You can't just change your mind!"

When the parent of an LGBTQIA+ individual comes from a conservative faith background, the parent's journey generally involves a lot of research, reading, taking deep dives, and talking to other LGBTQIA+ families and queer individuals about their experiences.

New information breeds new ways of viewing a situation and ignites more curiosity. We ask, "What else do I not know, or what may I have missed?"

When we have new information, it's a given that we will shift the way we view something—because our understanding has shifted! Sometimes this means we change our minds.

And it's not so much a *changing* of our mind that occurs as it is an assimilation of new information into "older," long-held beliefs and then EXPANDING our mind. We are seeing our circumstances through new eyes, new lenses.

So yes.

The answer is yes, actually, you *can* change your mind. To say that you cannot change your mind is binary thinking.

It's also important to note the role of consent when re-evaluating decisions you made earlier in life and whether or not you had sufficient information to *exercise* informed consent at that time. Maybe you feel you really did act with informed consent, but that doesn't mean you should ignore or dismiss new information, insight, and understandings as they come.

This is what makes us the higher species. We have the ability to absorb information and reason it out. We can weigh the pros and cons and evaluate them and our own thinking about the topic and then adjust our lives, behavior, and beliefs accordingly when we deem it needful or for our higher good.

Why are we so afraid of change?

I propose that the emotions we will have to feel to navigate change are underlying any resistance to or avoidance of change. That's because we do not want to experience the discomfort that comes along with change. We don't know how to feel our feelings because we have not been taught to. In the same way that we have physical energy that needs to be expended in some way, we have emotional energy that needs to be used, and we're not good at turning that energy into a productive fuel.

Perhaps you have experienced this in some way. It might look like avoiding a situation or person, or resisting taking that next step that you *know* you need to take.

Maybe it is remaining in denial about what is already going on around you or seems inevitable.

For example, your child may be graduating high school and it seems inevitable that they will be going off to college and having the opportunity to try out adulting for the first time.

Fear of change could be gripping you. Feeling fear about something is an invitation to pause and increase awareness around the fear.

Answer the following questions:

What is bringing up the fear for you?

What thoughts do you have when you're afraid of (fill in the blank)?

The purpose of this exercise is to show that there is *something* fueling the fear.

- Beliefs,
- opinions,
- stories, and
- thoughts

create our feelings.

The following analogy will help you tease out, loosen, and eventually dissolve the story. There is no shortage of stories, especially surrounding the topic of faith journeys.

A journey of faith doesn't fit inside a one-room schoolhouse.

Part 1: Starting your faith journey in the one-room schoolhouse

Centuries ago, instruction and learning wasn't available to all. But when it was available, it often took place in a one-room schoolhouse. Inside the schoolhouse were rows of either one-sized desks or tables matched up with benches, one chalkboard, one-sized slates upon which the pupils would write letters and numbers, one teacher, and one curriculum (that was purportedly that of the teacher and whatever higher institution of learning from which the teacher received their degree).

All students were thrown into the same one-room schoolhouse regardless of age, height, weight, family, sex, gender, or knowledge level. One unfortunate group was excluded: we know from history that students were "sorted" based on differences in race (color of skin). Although not the focus of this chapter, I mention it here to acknowledge this gross inequity in education.

In this one-room schoolhouse, I am sure much learning took place. And, there were limits. A student was able to learn from only the materials available and approved of by the know-how of one teacher. Perhaps younger students learned from other older students. Of course, all students had their own insights, but depending on whether sharing insights was celebrated or not, the students may or may not have kept those to themselves.

For those of a conservative faith background, a faith journey often begins in a building, a one-room schoolhouse of sorts. The students in this building are at all different places of learning and understanding. Folks are taught and learn from the materials available, and approved of, from the know-how of the "teacher."

They may learn from other pupils in the one-room schoolhouse and have their own insights, but if their insight is not celebrated, they most likely will keep it to themselves.

Part 2: A journey of faith doesn't fit inside a one-room schoolhouse.

<u>The stages of faith</u>

In the performing arts, performers usually climb steps of varying numbers to stand atop a stage—a platform upon which they demonstrate a certain know-how, skill, or talent. Sometimes the stage is shared, and other times the performer is solo.

There are various types of stages, from the elementary school stage used for the Christmas play all the way up to Carnegie Hall and beyond, with many others in between.

In the school of life, we could say the one-room schoolhouse is a stage. It is one stage—or step—in the grand staircase of learning. If we stay at (or in) the one-room schoolhouse step, that is where we will remain in knowledge, learning, and understanding.

The one-room schoolhouse has finite offerings. There is a reason society, or communities, no longer instruct pupils in one-room schoolhouses.

What if we start to realize that we don't "fit" inside the one-room schoolhouse any longer? What does that feel or look like?

Start by ASKING those whose knees have outgrown the desks or who have run out of space to write on their slate their learning, understanding, questions, and desires for more—more insight, more information, more growth. Just *more*.

On a faith journey, there are many stages or steps.

Imagine a staircase without beginning or end,

a staircase of tiny stages

that could be compared to

steps of understanding,

points of information,

levels of knowing,

courses of instruction,

rungs of inspiration,

places of being.

Part 3 - The journey of faith beyond the one-room schoolhouse

Not only have you *noticed* that you feel cramped, you begin to *acknowledge it*. It is your reality. You cannot deny it; to do so would be submitting yourself to a sentence of discomfort, living ill at ease, in cognitive dissonance and unhappiness, and sacrificing the possibility of self-fulfillment and true joy.

Alternatively, to acknowledge and act on what you have come to see as your reality doesn't mean the great beyond—the unknown—WILL be comfortable, full of ease and happiness, and rid you of the excruciating cognitive dissonance. But moving toward the unknown does bring the promise of hope, and the great WHAT IFs offer potential endless possibilities. (Incidentally, *ENDLESS* is another name for GOD.) It is expansive in all ways; this isn't a 2D pane or 3D cube. This is God's unending dimension.

Part 4 - Graduating from the one-room schoolhouse

You decide to venture out to some of the steps that lead outside the one-room schoolhouse. You begin to see that there is infinite room at each step or stage.

Sometimes, you'll find yourself alone on a step or stage, and other times with other travelers on your stages-of-faith journey.

We all have our own, personalized gear on this personal journey. We travel in different vehicles: on foot, bicycle, motorbike, a ship, in a car, high-passenger bus, or airplane. And our backpacks have contents specific to our journey: clothing, food, utensils, tools, extras like pain meds or prescriptions, items to help counter the environment like sunblock, a hat, goggles or glasses, gloves, and moleskin.

Some travelers were born with these provisions, others were given them, and still others will never have them or the opportunity to obtain them. Eventually, it may be decided that certain provisions are not needed.

Not everyone will feel like they don't fit in the one-room schoolhouse. Not everyone will want to venture beyond. That is OK. What is not OK is judging, shaming, belittling, or dismissing another's journey, including their step of graduating from the one-room schoolhouse.

Acceptance of another's journey can only happen when we lean into, rather than resist, change. Outcomes cannot be forced. Lack of control over them must be acknowledged and released, and then reality must be embraced.

Pulling an oracle card as part of my writing practice has become a meaningful way to receive "Divine downloads." Some of these Divine downloads have been so potent, deep, and profound. I love this part of writing.

At the end of 2023, after pulling a card, I received the message "to nurture that which you hold dear." In that message, I heard that I could keep the parts of "religion" that have helped me cultivate a relationship and connection with the Divine, or Higher Power, and simultaneously LET GO (or RELEASE) those things which were impeding and actively harming me or others.

I heard the question rise to the surface, "It can be BOTH/AND, right?" Yes, I learned that it can and that it must.

It has been my experience that when I keep the parts that resonate and let go of the parts that do not, a *new* space opens up for me. The best way I can describe it is that the energy that *was* tied up in the mental gymnastics of trying to make myself *or* my beliefs fit, or worrying what others may think or say, is now released from bondage and available to me.

This new space is filled with an expansive energy, one of possibility. I have purposely chosen to live in the space of both/and. My kiddo identifies as transgender, so the traditional metaphors and analogies really don't apply. There's no table or chairs for those who identify as transgender or nonbinary. The patriarchy would have to totally dissolve to make room for them.

I can't afford to emotionally, mentally, or spiritually invest in hope that the patriarchy will do that, not right now anyway. So, I am at a place where I completely define my faith journey, and honestly it evolves daily. And I give myself 100% permission to allow that evolution and embrace that aspect of my journey.

September 3, 2024

I drove all day yesterday on my way home from Flagstaff, AZ after dropping AJ off at Northern Arizona University. Solo driving is exhausting.

Last night, on the final leg of my two-day journey, I made a stop on the west side of Fort Worth. I was an hour from home, and I wasn't feeling well, but nothing was going to get in my way of seeing my dear friend Jeanie. Although getting together at Starbucks was only our second time meeting in person, I felt connected to Jeanie from the day I interviewed her for my podcast in the Fall of 2023.

Like me, Jeanie is the mother of a transgender son. From our first conversation, I learned that I can talk with her about pretty much anything.

Last night, we talked about where we were on our faith journeys. We commiserated over our hurt and angry feelings regarding the recent policy changes made in the handbook of our faith of origin (LDS) that specifically affected transgender individuals. We swapped stories of how life was going in general for our families and specifically our transgender kiddos.

At one point, Jeanie paused very pronouncedly, and asked, "Do you have a grandfather? That you are close to? I'm getting something very strongly," pointing to her head and heart simultaneously.

It was at that moment that I remembered! The lightbulb in my brain went back on!

That's right, I thought, *she has this gift! Jeanie has this beautiful gift of being so close to our angels. She senses them and can hear them speaking to her all. the. time.*

Now I was on the edge of my seat wanting to know what she was going to share next!

I answered her, slowly, a little perplexed.

I said, "Well . . . my Grandpa Burnham—my mom's dad—died in the nineties; I knew him some. My other grandpa, Grandpa Schultz, was the last of my four grandparents to pass away—in 2017. I became somewhat closer to him over the years. He was from Texas, so we had that in common."

Even though I was born in Arizona, I've lived in Texas more than any other place in my life—nineteen months as a church missionary, and as a married adult I've lived here since 2004. Both of my kids have been raised here and are basically Texans. My Grandpa Schultz loved Texas (incidentally, Grandma Betty hated Texas, but that's another story).

In my response to Jeanie, I then added, "But his wife, my Grandma Betty, is really who I was closer to. Of all my grandparents, I was closest to her. I was the oldest granddaughter, and my older brother was the oldest grandson. My dad was their oldest child, so my brother and I were the first grandkids. My dad's younger brothers were more like older brothers to me."

Jeanie apologized.

She kind of stammered as she said, "This is weird. Is it weird that I'm asking all these questions? It's just that someone is bonking me on the head! They really want me to share this message with you."

I emphatically shook my head. "No! Not at all! You have a beautiful gift. I want to know what you have to share."

Jeanie and I have only met in person one other time. We first found one another online in a Facebook group for parents (with an LDS background) who have queer kids. We connected because of and through our mutual understanding of being mothers of transgender kids. She even bravely came on my podcast and shared her and her transgender son's story.

Jeanie continued, hesitantly, "What is AJ's birth name?"

I froze. I couldn't believe it. I had never told Jeanie my kiddo's birth name. I was stunned Jeanie had thought to ask me this. Not in an offensive way, but rather, I knew there was something very real and potent happening with our conversation.

I answered Jeanie as tears were welling up in my eyes. "Actually, I named him after my Grandma Betty. A few years ago, he decided he would legally change his middle name to James, and that's OK. It's all good."

I had genuinely done the internal work to come to a point where I felt my grandma was OK with that; I felt comfortable in my kiddo desiring that change.

The only other people who knew I had named my kiddo after my Grandma Betty were family members. Actually, several other great-grandchildren had also been named after Grandma Betty. She was a beloved grandmother. I always felt special and deeply loved in her presence, even when she responded with, "I don't believe in that stuff" when I shared that I had been accepted to and was starting graduate school in School Counseling Psychology at BYU. I knew her response was largely due to the generation she grew up in. The "silent generation" didn't understand so much of what we have as common knowledge in the social sciences now. There was much more unknown than known in her time.

Jeanie said, "I know you need to get going, but they want you to know they are cheering you on! They are so proud of you and AJ! As a matter of fact, do you like music?" (yes!) "They want you to listen to music on the rest of your way home! Music that will energize and uplift. And do you like baths?" (also yes!) "Take a hot bubble bath when you get home!"

WOW. Just wow.

I would have shortchanged myself of this experience if I had not made the effort to begin to learn to speak up, to share my truth.

Anyone can talk to another person. To speak up and share your truth, your heart, your experience shifts energy strong enough to move mountains. It did, and continues to for me. THIS is the foundation of change, renewal, and rebirth.

A rebirth or renewal cannot occur before the contraction and release that comes with change, just like a resurrection cannot come before a surrendering.

This is transience.

TransparentSEE

6

TRANSDUCTION

(the process of accepting energy in one form and giving back related energy in a different form)

But all those pretty pictures they just start to fade away
And everything that I believed is getting hard to find
Have I lost the only one
Who ever felt like mine

———

I was taught to always turn the other cheek
But you know I took a beatin' and I stayed up on my feet
And this faith is gettin' heavy but you know it carries me
To the streets, to the river
Where the broken dreams flow out into the sea

I keep on looking but something's always missing
I keep on looking for something bigger than me
From the saints to the sinners all the losers and the winners
Yeah, we're all just looking for something
Something to believe in

———

I'm tired of sleeping
Sleeping through my own life
It's time to wake up
Wake up with eyes open wide
I'm tired of sleeping
Sleeping through my own life
It's time to wake up with arms open wide

> ~ "Caught in the Storm," recorded by Goo Goo Dolls,
> written by John Rzeznik and John Shanks

November 23, 2024

The more I release myself from the thoughts that grip me, the beliefs that bind me . . . the more I can feel myself breathe, the more I can feel myself open up, the more I am able to allow love and expansion into my mind, heart, soul, being, essence.

I chatted with my coach Minda again yesterday morning. I have been remembering something she said on our call a couple weeks ago.

"You are never alone. You always have your guides, your angels, and Spirit with you."

I have been thinking about that a lot. As I lean more and more into that belief, I think I can actually see the fruits of it. I have been paying more attention as well.

Having an outside perspective helps me to lighten up about life's circumstances in general. It offers fresh eyes and even adds some humor to the situation as I look at it from a more objective vantage point. Humor is healing. It reminds us that we are human and that we don't have to take ourselves so seriously.

To take ourselves seriously comes from a place of fear. When you tease at what is underlying the fear, you can begin to loosen and observe it, invite curiosity into your view, then feel or metabolize it, and release the fear.

The only way to liberate your being from fear is to feel it in your body. You must allow the energy of the fear to transform you as you metabolize and alchemize it—using that energy as you burn that fuel in healthy ways.

Fear is sometimes masked by anger: anger that things are not going to plan, or the unexpected is now staring you in the face, or you have been hurt or betrayed and you do not know what to do, nor do you want to try to figure it out. Fear masked by anger often calls shotgun, compounding the feeling that you've lost control of the situation.

When we realize that the feeling of "losing control" is a lie—because we really never had control to begin with—we can begin to heal from the energetic part of the emotion that is causing us pain and suffering. The idea that we "have control" over anything is resistance to surrendering to what actually exists and what is *meant* for us.

We must ask and be willing to answer, "What is the wound under the surface that is creating the fear I am masking as anger?" And, "What can I learn from the messages offered by this wound?" (Messages = the thoughts we have about the wound.)

The reality is, when anger is copilot, most likely we have released choosing our words and actions from a purposeful, constructive place. We are not in creation energy.

Anytime we speak or act (or don't speak or act) from a place of anger, we create the opposite of what both parties need: instead of being seen, heard, and loved, it is more probable they feel invisible, discounted, and dismissed.

Anger doesn't have to be a problem. The *presence* of fear isn't a problem. It is the expression driven by anger and our actions that come from a place of fear that *can* make matters worse. Actions that hurt others, betray trust, cause damage, or create suffering are detrimental.

Acting from anger completely ignores and negates the *active* role of hope. Action driven by fear skips and denies the need for struggle. When we give in to fear and anger in that space between the stimulus and response, we miss out on nurturing and building mental and emotional muscles. We deny ourselves the moment to be taught, to choose what we want to create and the emotion necessary to create it. It takes time to shovel, rake, and hoe the many rows of thought found in the garden of neuroplasticity in the brain.

There is only one alternative: in that space between stimulus and response, we must pause, listen, invite curiosity, and ask.

Ask our fear what it is trying to teach us. Why is it present? Listen to the messages sent by anger alerting us of unmet needs, injustices, and calls for change. What are they trying to protect us from that is actually already safe?

How do you define hope? How about struggle?

For the word *hope*, I like to look to the Spanish language. In Spanish, *esperanza* means "hope" and comes from the infinitive *esperar* which means "to hope or to wait for." The roots of the word come from Old English *hopian*, meaning "to wish, expect, look forward (to something)." This is active.

Therefore, hope is a *feeling of expectation giving us permission to dream for a better tomorrow.*

I like to use the word *wrestle* to best describe the idea of a struggle.

A wrestle is an ongoing process, a push-and-pull dynamic, an expanding and contracting. This process ultimately has the potential to birth new life and energy, or create a rebirth that reframes our life or energy.

I believe we can't have hope without struggle. I have found hope is a function of struggle. Waiting is a part of both.

I have asked myself the question, *How do I have hope in Christ, or anything, without some sort of struggle?*

From a spiritual lens, it's not realistic or possible to experience the exhilarating highs of hope without the depths, sometimes depleting lows, of struggle. How can we allow struggle if we don't acknowledge and make room for the visceral tension existing between two opposing forces, an organic occurrence that accompanies struggle?

I don't believe it is possible; the palpable tension between two opposing forces is requisite. We find tension in many places, two of which are paradox and opposition. Paradox exists when our lived experience is different from beliefs we've been taught or had handed down to us. And we have seen opposition as a negative thing for far too long. I now see it as a natural tension, the fuel of a push-and-pull of energy that helps humanity go forward.

Consider the process involved in driving a car.

> Engines have pistons that move up and down inside metal tubes called cylinders. Imagine riding a bicycle: Your legs move up and down to turn the pedals. Pistons are connected via rods (they're like your shins) to a crankshaft, and they move up and down to spin the engine's crankshaft, the same way your legs spin the bike's—which in turn powers the bike's drive wheel or car's drive wheels.[9]

Opposition propels humanity forward akin to the transmission of a car transferring power from the engine to the

---

[9] Source: https://www.caranddriver.com/features/a26962316/how-a-car-works/

wheels, making it possible for the vehicle to go. This fuels—sends energy to—the wheels, which in turn provide the function allowing the car to go places.

In what shape is your engine? Is it healthy enough to create the power needed to be transferred to the other parts of the body to make tracks and go? Is it able to increase power—speed—if needed?

The more I lean into my truth, the stronger I feel, the less resistance I exert, and the easier and more natural this process becomes.

And there is absolutely no turning back.

Does a snake who has molten and shed an old layer of skin seek to refit it once more? No, that is absurd. Once the old layer is released and allowed to peel off, it cannot be put back on again. The whole point of shedding the skin is to prepare for a new, more expanded stage of growth. And besides, the skin no longer fits.

The molting and releasing process reveals a new, fresh layer of skin. This layer has never existed nor been seen before, and is now taking the place of the old. And the new skin is better suited for growth.

And such is the human mind.

> "Every now and then a man's mind is stretched by a new idea or sensation, and never shrinks back to its former dimensions."[10]

Like the rays of the sun stretching out over the horizon at day's beginning, once a new vista makes an appearance on the horizon of the human psyche, it cannot go back from whence it came. It's not physically possible for the sunrays, nor intellectually possible for the point of view, to vanish.

And if it *were* possible, what would be the point of it?

---

[10] Oliver Wendell Holmes, *The Autocrat of the Breakfast Table, Volume I*, p.266

Why would the sunlight revert back under the horizon where it can no longer shine and shed light on humanity? And why would the human mind want to put away another kind of new light and understanding and push it into the depths of the psyche to be forgotten, shunned, denied, and then replaced with shame at its mere mention?

I assert there would be no point, no advantage, no expansion. Shame is a false persona that tries to crowd inside our being—our true self—but it can only reside within us with permission. Shame clouds vision and masks reality.

I believe seeing past the shame to new light and understanding is what motivated Eve to make her choice to eat the apple in the Garden of Eden. Once Eve made her choice, she was not able to turn back, but I don't believe she wanted to because she knew what was *meant for her*. She knew that she would be leaving the Garden of Eden, regardless of what Adam decided. She would not have made the choice to eat the apple without thinking it through; a choice of that magnitude would not have been made lightly.

What are the "apples" in your life? When have you made a choice to "eat of the fruit" knowing that there is no turning back? This is a choice that you know to your very core; even if the option were available, you would not turn back.

Perhaps it is outside of your awareness that the option is available to you to take a bite of the apple, so you haven't yet given yourself permission. Shame often stands in the way of giving ourselves permission.

> "Awareness without self-compassion can create so much shame."[11]

---

[11] Mary Wall, fellow coach

Shame is an emotion attached to our stories about ourselves, our family, upbringing, background, and choices. The deeper shame is buried, the longer it's ignored, the more it grows, festers, and worsens. Shame thrives in environments where there is no emotional, mental, or spiritual safety.

To dissolve the shame, you must speak your story—share your experiences—in the presence of an empathetic witness. A friend, coach, or therapist in a one-on-one or group setting can provide this space.

I always say, "Shame has no power in the face of authenticity." You get to choose with whom and where you show up authentically, and how much of your authenticity you share. Confidentiality is nonnegotiable to ensure safety and foster trust in this process. This takes the energy of shame and turns it into something positive and beautiful while simultaneously turning it on its head, challenging and rewriting it.

We don't talk about this enough.

Shame, coupled with conditioned binary thinking, doesn't allow permission to ask the hard questions. Self-compassion, releasing shame attached to our stories, inviting questions, and adding curiosity are the recipe for evolution, learning, and expansion.

What IF Adam had declined to partake of the fruit?

What if Eve had had to leave alone?

What does that mean about Eve? About Adam?

What does this teach us?

What can we learn and apply in the present day from this biblical story and perspective?

I'm not interested in debating whether or not these stories are historically accurate or embellished fiction. I believe lessons can be learned regardless.

I want to celebrate the BOTH/AND!

Can we celebrate that Eve both made her choice *and* allowed the consequences to follow, including releasing the outcome of what Adam would decide? Let's celebrate that the potential consequences could both be good *and* present challenges, growth opportunities, and perhaps even heartache.

Can we also celebrate that Adam acted as a free agent, listened to Eve, considered her words, *and then* also made his choice?

Can we celebrate the messy and the beautiful? I believe we can, and we need to.

> "There are times when we need to learn to hold two opposing beliefs or ideas at the same time. We resist the contradictory nature of it, but being able to tolerate both at the same time is transformational."[12]

In another biblical story, the wife of Lot gets a bad wrap for having turned to look back at the city of Sodom and Gomorrah as it was being destroyed. Do you blame her? This was home, her safe place, the place tied to memories.

Is it not the most human of human emotions to long for something? To ache for what was? To hope and want something that is just out of reach, that seems so close but is far away?

It is in the push-and-pull forces of longing, aching, hoping, and reaching that we allow ourselves the fullness and richness of this human experience. It is the expanding and contracting of our minds and hearts that make it possible to tolerate contradiction and dissonance, feel our fear, and allow the anger to teach, and then act productively. As we ask questions of our fear and anger, we learn what is whispering below the surface.

Those whispers call our attention to the apples meant for us, those of which we must partake. This is no low-hanging fruit. They are found among the very high-hanging fruit. The act of partaking

---

[12] Andelin Price, fellow coach

of our fruit initiates metabolism. This energy is alchemized into a new, higher and holier form. It amplifies the voice within, calling us to act for the marginalized voices without, increase equity and equality, cultivate belonging, and call out injustices.

This is transduction.

7

TRANSLATION/ TRANSCRIPTION

(express the sense [of words or text] in another language; emotions as a foreign language)

So this is what the truth feels like
This is more of what I had in mind
Yeah, this is what the truth feels like
And I'm feeling it, I'm feeling it

———

Oh, it's unexplainable and it's so weird
Woah, it's so strange, confusing and I'm so scared.

~ "This Is What the Truth Feels Like,"
recorded by Gwen Stefani, written by Gwen Stefani, Julia
Michaels, Justin Tranter, Mattias Per Larsson, and Robin
Lennart Fredriksson

March 10, 2024

I grew up when everything was corded, attached, and came with some sort of stipulations or conditions. *Everything* was tethered in some way.

Car keys: the only way to turn on a car was to turn over the correct, physical, metal key in the ignition.

Door keys: ever heard of latchkey kids?

Telephones: the house had to be wired with telephone wiring first, so the phone attached to the wall, either directly or with a phone cord such that it had a place for the signal to travel.

Computers: literally plugged into the wall. And all the accessories plugged into the computer—the hard drive, the printer, and any other add-ons like external drives.

Cash: although prototypes were introduced in the late 1960s, ATMs weren't common until the '80s.

Cash registers: plugged into the wall, but they were at least electronic and the buttons beeped with each push.

There was no such thing as swipe, insert, or tap-to-pay. We had those dinosaur plastic trays (manual imprinter) to place the rectangular double receipt over the plastic credit card, a copy each for merchant and customer. One or two manual swipes requiring some muscle would pick up the sixteen raised digits of the credit card. Later, when the night manager closed out, they could tally them manually to be included in the day's sales and mail the merchant copy to the bank for deposit.

Radios: connected to the socket in the wall and subject to the fine-tuning of the physical round dial.

Televisions: plugged into the wall with a hope and a prayer that you could find the sweet spot for the bunny ears on top to pick up the strongest transmission.

Movies: you could only see them in theaters; VCRs weren't common until the later '0s.

Grocery stores: nowadays, it's optional to go in person; the store literally comes to you.

Women: in the form of bank accounts, loans, credit cards, ownership of property [none were allotted to women without a male cosigner.]. It's no wonder there are many who are tired.

There was no staying on a phone call while jumping into your car to head to your next appointment or run errands. You couldn't catch up on episodes of your favorite show or Marco Polo a friend while making dinner. You literally had no choice but to move at a slower pace.

Nowadays, our brains are "rewiring" on an almost daily basis. How many versions of things in life have Gen-Xers learned that they have had to "update?" Regularly. More than once.

With the faster pace that comes with "updates" (ability to multitask) comes the expectation to do more with the "extra" time. Downtime is not viewed as needed or valuable.

Sometimes there's a bug in the updates that we're supposed to learn (download). Sometimes the newer, updated version isn't compatible.

For instance . . .

I don't know how to find God anymore. It's not like there's a busy signal. I can't even find a dial tone. I try to hold on to the line, then fruitlessly and repeatedly push the hangup button over and over. I find myself tapping and shaking the phone, violently trying to get a dial tone and ultimately to find connection. And that's when I realize . . .

The line is dead.

I don't know exactly when it went dead, but it's dead. Gone. It occurs to me that my outdated system is not compatible with this new software I've been given in life.

I try to move forward anyway, in some way, put on the façade that is expected of me, that everything is OK. Isn't that what we're supposed to do? Except, it's not. Then I just feel like an effing fraud.

Nothing is OK.

I came to realize communication was getting lost in translation. It was time to learn a new language. I was about to meet a new teacher. Keira Brinton is a big part of the reason I regained a belief in God, the Divine, a Power greater than us all.

The one thing I never expected but have definitely experienced on this journey is feeling like the cord between me and my connection with the Divine was pulled. No, it was severed. I felt that severance and bled for a while. Folks don't talk about emotional, mental, or spiritual pain as much as they do physical, but it is *visceral,* and it is real.

Have you ever noticed that what we think we don't want in life comes in the form of questions? Case in point: questions I ask myself often:

What is the point of all this anyway?

Why is this still happening to me?

Who am I to do this thing?

What is the purpose in all of these deep emotions I feel and ride that come and go just like the waves until they crash upon the shore?

Why must they be so very deep, to the point of debilitation?

Why does no one else see what I see in my faith of origin?

Why did/does no one else "wake up" and see what has been plaguing women for centuries? (That sounds like a lot of judgment on my part, I know.)

Why do I have to be the one to speak up?

Why doesn't my [insert relationship here] speak up?

December 5, 2023

I need to acknowledge myself. See myself. Love myself.

My anger about my situation is consuming me. I have shut down. My shame has entered as it has in times past.

How do I release the anger and this harsh self-judgment?

I hear loudly and clearly: it's time. It's time to start writing my book. What does that even mean?

Writing my book . . . really, it means putting my story into words such that it is shareable with others, so that it might touch others.

89

I have learned to keep it all inside. Some—a lot—of the anger comes from not being seen by others in my faith community, which by nature includes my family.

I feel invisible.

I feel that by continuing to attend church I am choosing to remain in a relationship where I am verbally and emotionally abused.

Why is it so hard to walk away?

Do I need to walk away?

And there it is . . . I retrace my steps back a paragraph where I wrote a question. What I thought I didn't want in life came in the form of a question: **how do I release the anger and this harsh self-judgment?**

And the answer I hear deep inside is clear:

Maybe I don't release the anger. Maybe I channel it. Perhaps I don't let go of the harsh self-judgment but rather I transform it.

When I wrote that December journal entry, I was sort of angry about *not* holding on to the anger, and yet intrigued enough to entertain the thoughts. But, I had no clue how to channel the anger and transform the self-judgment.

Emotional and mental health are related but markedly different. To cope with life and relations well, we must balance our thoughts and emotions. If we are out of sorts, one or the other (mental or emotional health) will be impacted. Understanding how to restore balance is the key to resilience and a higher quality of life.

So, what is mental health? It is the hardware of the brain, and emotional health is the software. Mental health is about the functioning of the brain, which includes emotional, intellectual, spiritual, and social health.

Among other things, mental health determines our ability to reason: how we handle decision-making, process information, interact with others, and manage stress. When we encounter mental health challenges, these basic functions are impacted.

Emotional health is more about the feelings evoked by the information we process. Elements of emotional health include having awareness of emotions in the first place, accepting and allowing them, processing and managing them, and expressing them in healthy ways.

> "The main difference between mental and emotional health is that mental health involves processing information, storing it in memory, and understanding this information while emotional health involves the ability to control and express emotions."[13]

Although I like this description, I now believe emotional health is not about controlling our emotions as much as it is about allowing, feeling, metabolizing, and processing them. The ability to *feel* our emotions is a modern concept. More accurately, *awareness around tolerating the discomfort* of truly "feeling our emotions" is a novel concept in the present day. When I use the word "ability," I mean developing that muscle to not just tolerate but eventually appreciate all the emotions.

I no longer qualify emotions as bad or good, or positive or negative. I see them as teachers offering insight and information. This is definitely not something that my generation or the ones before were taught, and we were certainly never encouraged to *feel* our emotions.

This is especially true of anger. *Feeling* the emotion of anger was discouraged, shamed, and even classified (with contention) as being "of the devil," as if we could control our feelings. Fixating on *controlling* completely shifts the focus from feeling the feeling to

---

[13] Hasa, "Difference between Mental and Emotional Health," April 22, 2020, https://pediaa.com/difference-between-mental-and-emotional-health/.

trying to manipulate, change, get rid of, ignore, or hide it. That is a losing battle.

Alternatively, when we are able to view our emotions from a neutral lens, we enter a space of openness and expansion. When we pause and allow ourselves to feel, the space we create in that moment allows our hearts, minds, spirits, and souls to be taught the needs behind our emotions.

Emotions are teachers. They have messages to share and lessons to teach. They are the green flags that alert us to needs not currently in our lens of awareness.

The trick is to learn to catch the green flags.

> "Between stimulus and response there is a space. In
> that space is our power to choose our response. In
> our response lies our growth and freedom."[14]

The green flags are found in that space between stimulus and response. Even before we are aware of our thoughts that accompany the stimulus (event, situation, words spoken, action done), we *feel* something. More often than not, it is the *emotion* we notice first.

There is your green flag. That is your cue to pause, reflect, and listen.

I ask, "Are you listening?"

"Yes," you say.

I clarify, "Who is listening?"

"Me," you say.

I offer that, actually, the voice who just answered "me" is the one listening. Your power lies within that voice. It is where your Inner Knowing can be found. It is there, and has been all along.

---

[14] Quoted by Stephen R. Covey in the Foreword of *Lead or Get Off the Pot!* by Pat Croce (Covey did not specify the name of the original source).

Only, it gets smothered every time you try to negate, ignore, bury, deny, manipulate, change, or force a feeling.

Our words and actions are birthed from our feelings. When our feelings die, a premature death of mind and soul is expedited. This is a pain so deep and profound, it is soul harrowing. This is suffering—emotional, mental, and spiritual pain.

The physical and emotional discomfort of *allowing* a feeling like anger far outweighs the suffering that accompanies long-term denial or burial, all while it continues to build *because it's* being pushed down. It's like the grease-stained dust rag in the corner of the garage on the verge of spontaneous, enormous combustion.

One day in the fall of 2024, I met my new friend Emmaly Renshaw. A director in the agricultural nonprofit sector, Emmaly specializes in urban agriculture and urban food-system initiatives in Iowa. She agreed to share her story on my podcast, and I am so grateful she did. My heart was filled, my soul deeply touched, and my being foundationally shifted.

After serving many years in a stake leadership position for the LDS church (a significant responsibility overseeing nine to ten wards, or geographical congregations), she was released from her duties. With the release from that position, she felt her work over those years was all erased with the raise of a hand. Not long after being released, she had arrived at a point in her faith journey where she said, "I was exhausted. I could feel the anger start to seep when I read this book [called *Rage*] and realized that a lot of the anger I had was valid. But I didn't know where to put it, and I didn't have a place to set it down and sort it out."

It was during this time of deep reflection that her father called and asked her to come home to be an extra set of hands for the seasonal prescribed burn of their forty acres. In preparation for the main burn, there is first the time-consuming yet essential preburn called "backburning." This consists of starting a lot of smaller fires and then putting them out to create a boundary around which the main burn will ideally remain contained once the match is dropped. During our interview, Emmaly shared her experience with me.

> As I'm doing this process, leading a backburn crew, I related it to women. That's what we do: we see a fire and we're taught to extinguish it right away. There's never the ability to let it burn and to grow into anything larger.

> It's the same with anger. Anger has no place to go. If your anger flashes, [you're supposed] to tamper it down.

> I have daughters. As I'm in this backburn process, I started to understand I do the same to them. They come home from a rough day at school and there's drama and I'll be like, "Let's simmer down, let's take it down a notch . . ." [I was] realizing that I do the same thing to the next generation, where my home should be a place where they can set that fire and let it burn in a safe place.

> For that particular night, I had the opportunity to start the fire. When you drop a match and let it burn, I think there's an analogy that there comes a point where you know you don't have control over it anymore.

> The only thing that's going to keep that fire in line is your backburn. And I think a lot of that is like faith and anger.

> The opportunity to physically drop the match in a field is exhilarating, and it's also a lot of responsibility. I thought about a lot of times, as women in the church, we do the fields burn. But it's

typically one person . . . that lights the match and is out there and burns the field.

When we look at this analogy and how we do prescribed burns: prescribed burns are a team effort. If you're one individual in a field with a match, you're an arsonist. But when you go in and you burn with a team and you have the communication you need to get those safety barriers in, it's no longer dangerous. It's helpful and it's healing.

And within the Church, we have women who know how to burn. Where we really struggle is, we don't teach other women the art of burning and how to do it correctly. A lot of times as we go through these transitions and life experiences, we don't share them out of fear.

From a distance, prescribed burns look terrifying. You have to call the fire department beforehand because they'll get dozens of calls. [Through] this experience, I've thought "How can we put our anger to work and not let it just simmer in our bodies and in the quiet spaces of our life?"

Fire does not have to be disastrous. It can be, [and] can do good. It's the prescribed burns, allowing things to burn on a particular schedule or regiment, [that] helps plants, and it helps weed control. [There is a] beautiful thing about prairie burns. We did this one in late April, and I returned in June, and there was no sign of the burner damage. The ecosystem had been completely replenished within eight weeks, and growth happened again.[15]

My friend Emmaly poetically demonstrated through her mesmerizingly beautiful narrative, **this** is the language of emotions. **These** are the green flags that invite us to pause, listen, and learn. Emotions are the teachers that transcribe our needs into readable code.

I went back to read my journal entry of December 5, 2023 and realized that I wrote:

I've been judging myself for feeling this anger and have been running from it.

Anger does not deserve the classification of a bad or undesirable emotion it has been given.

As a teacher, anger is masterful.

It forces me to acknowledge what I try to avoid.

It reminds me I'm alive as I feel the hot pulses sear through my body. They are electrical impulses at their basic level sending electric messages from synapse to synapse.

And underneath the electrical anger lies something deeper, more profound.

Upheaval.

Questioning.

---

[15] Emmaly Fenton Renshaw in an interview with the author on *Living Beyond the Shadow of Doubt* podcast, "Episode 144: The Art of Burning with Emmaly Radshaw," October 1, 2024.

Sadness.

Loss.

Uncertainty.

Invisibility.

Sorrow.

Mourning.

Death.

Death of certainty, community, dreams, belonging, expectations, familiarity.

Akin to the life cycle of a Phoenix, I've learned that with death assuredly comes rebirth. Not one, nor two, or three . . . but infinite rebirths— but not before the transformative power death lays claim to our soul on a molecular level through the process of "dying."

Micro processes and macro processes.

It is unavoidable, and now I know I would not have wanted to avoid it, for to avoid it would mean the avoidance of living and life itself.

Energy needs a container to change form. My body is my container. The energy within that I feel simultaneously with emotion (energy in motion) is transforming and ever evolving.

Always.

Anger is a teacher.

This is translation.

TransparentSEE

TRANSFORMATION

(the act of changing the form of; "transform," by the 1550s, was defined as "change the nature, character, or disposition of"[16])

I'm bleeding out
So if the last thing that I do
Is bring you down
I'll bleed out for you

So I bare my skin
And I count my sins
And I close my eyes
And I take it in
I'm bleeding out
I'm bleeding out for you

When the day has come
That I've lost my way around
And the seasons stop

---

[16] https://www.etymonline.com/word/transform

And hide beneath the ground
When the sky turns gray
And everything is screaming
I will reach inside
Just to find my heart is beating

———

When the hour is nigh
And hopelessness is sinking in
And the wolves all cry
To fill the night with hollering
When your eyes are red
And emptiness is all you know
With the darkness fed
I will be your scarecrow

You tell me to hold on
Oh, you tell me to hold on
But innocence is gone
And what was right is wrong

'Cause I'm bleeding out
So if the last thing that I do
Is bring you down
I'll bleed out for you.

> ~ "Bleeding Out," Recorded by Imagine Dragons,
> written by Alexander Junior Grant, Benjamin Arthur
> Mckee, Daniel Coulter Reynolds, Daniel Wayne Sermon,
> and Joshua Francis Mosser

Stories entertain us.

Some soothe and calm us to help us slow down at day's end.

Others pass on a legacy or record history from our progenitors to our descendants.

December 19, 2023

Affirmation: I can feel discomfort safely.

I realized yesterday that I found myself smack in the middle of my "story-ness." It's a story I've known for a long time . . . I'm alone, not good enough, don't fit in, there's not a place for me in faith community or community in general, in my family, etc.

This usually happens surrounding anything having to do with the church. I had just watched a missionary homecoming talk via Zoom on Sunday. Abi was gone with a friend for the day; Aves and I drove to get a soda. And per usual on Sundays, I was feeling "alone."

I had a moment yesterday morning (Monday) where I paused and realized, "Wait, I don't have to listen to this crap. I don't have to take this emotional abuse from myself. Why do I continue to do so?"

It was really powerful, and in a split moment I could feel CHOICE involved. I could sense and opt for a choice in how I proceeded forward.

Why do I continue to listen to voices and their messages I would never dream of using with friends or family? It would be so discouraging!

All of us are operating from a place of the stories we've unconsciously written, the imprints made on our psyche during childhood and beyond. Most don't recognize these as the stories they are and are not able to distinguish themselves and live a life separate from these stories.

Not only do we have stories about us stemming from childhood and beyond, we have stories about others in our lives. Here are others of mine that I have created.

Spouse

He hasn't been OK with and won't approve of or accept where my faith journey is taking me in this evolution I'm experiencing as my eyes are opening.

Kids

I don't know what to teach them as I am trying to figure things out for myself. Will lack of teaching be worse than teaching what I've been taught?

Parents

I can never tell them about the shifts that have occurred in me; it would break their baby-boomer hearts. They have given all to this church, and their identity is based in it. I think it would crush them.

Siblings

They're going to think Meagan is falling away. I don't think they'll want me around their kids—I'm a bad influence.

Nieces, nephews, and niblings (nonbinary or trans kiddos of one's siblings)

They may not believe in the Divine at all if I speak my truth of where I am at in my faith journey. (Now I choose to reframe that story as: they will see me in my truth and see that I am human— simultaneously lovable, curious, and messy.)

BFF

She is not OK with this; we are drifting apart.

Faith community members

I already didn't feel like I truly belonged or that I was "one of them." This will only serve to deepen and widen that divide.

Nuanced faith members

They will distance themselves because my words and actions are triggering them. It's like perhaps they want to do or say the same as me but aren't there yet, so they move away.

Former members of my faith community

They are judging me because I am not navigating this the "right way" or the way they did.

Neighbors across and down the street

When I'm contemplating putting up a rainbow flag in my front yard, even a garden sized one, I believe they will see us as woke, progressive, or radicals and not want to associate with us.

Civic and school community

I served on the PTA for many years—the majority of my kids' schooling years. The town has grown a lot, but at one point I knew everyone and they knew me. My story: they are judging me from afar, finding evidence for why it was OK for them to distance themselves and their kids from my kiddo and our family. Likewise, my family and I are judging them from afar, finding evidence for why it's OK to distance ourselves from them (or at least, I am doing that).

Please keep in mind, these are stories I created in my thoughts and the feelings of my heart during this hugely transitional and transformational time of my life.

I'm not saying they were reality.

Thoughts and feelings aren't *facts.*

But, these stories *felt* true because **I believed** them. There's value in the awareness of these stories: awareness equals information that affords me the opportunity to choose how to feel about these circumstances rather than being in a reactionary state, on autopilot from habitual thoughts.

With each of these relationships, something happened—an occurrence or experience to which I assigned meaning: I received a text message or phone call (or stopped receiving them); a youth or previous friend stopped reaching out to my kiddo; teachers did not honor or use preferred name or pronouns; parents (both in and out of our faith community) "warned" their children about my child; people at church did not immediately respond to my requests for more inclusion (or sometimes didn't respond at all). In many cases, I (or we) just didn't feel seen, heard, or loved.

According to Anna Aslanian, LMFT, CGT, with the Gottman institute:

1. Any experience that causes you to develop self-limiting and negative beliefs about yourself is trauma.

2. There are "big 'T' traumas," such as surviving wars, abuse, assault, natural disasters. And there are "small 't' traumas," which are conscious and subconscious hurtful experiences that haven't been processed. These are things like rejection, perceived failures, and breakups—pain that adds up. Pain that's normalized in our society.

3. Trauma is what happened, and it's also what should have happened that didn't.[17]

The stories we've created surrounding significant individuals in our lives can and often do result in what Anna describes as "little

---

[17] *Healing Old Wounds: How Childhood Attachment Trauma Shows up in our Relationships*, Gottman Institute Training Video

't' trauma." A need wasn't met, a mishap was not corrected, or a painful experience was not "righted" or at least apologized for.

I think there are misconceptions about how trauma is healed. For years, I believed that something major had to happen for trauma to heal, that it takes many years of massive effort, and even that it happened for other people but wasn't available to me.

I believe underlying this misconception was shame. The belief that we aren't good enough or worthy—we are inherently bad—is based in shame. Shame whispers the lie, "You aren't enough." The messages from shame are all lies.

Religious beliefs that teach that actions are directly tied to a person's value and worthiness are problematic. This approach takes little thought for the effects of trauma, and it fails to acknowledge that what may not be trauma-inducing for one individual may be for another.

Religious beliefs coupled with an emotional trauma response can become confusing. It was for me when I was a child. Because I didn't understand that the sexual abuse wasn't my fault, I carried a feeling of not being "enough"—not good enough, worthy enough, spiritual enough, righteous enough—all the way into adulthood. This "not enoughness" has been a recurring theme in my life.

Additionally, performative belief tenets fuel the idea that healing is merit-based and dependent upon one's faith and worthiness. For me, this idea placed the act or gift of healing *just out* of my reach. In my childlike view, to heal from physical or emotional pain, trauma resulting from the actions of others or even life circumstances—*any* reason for seeking healing—the evidence was there that it would take miracles and herculean effort. Miracles didn't happen to people like me; they happened to other folks or only occurred in biblical times.

When I was a child, healing and wholeness seemed impossible, and that belief affected my self-esteem and how I viewed myself—an effect that stayed with me well into adulthood.

Childhood abuses I suffered resulted in long-lasting guilt and shame, but I didn't realize they were not mine to carry. They were NEVER mine to begin with, but I didn't understand this nor did I know how to release them from my body, mind, heart, and soul.

I sincerely didn't understand.

I only began to see the truth—that I was already loved, worthy, and perfect (meaning *whole*)—when I started to deconstruct my deeply ingrained religious beliefs, which started when I learned my kiddo identified as queer.

Unfortunately, shame can be a cycle that we revisit again and again. There's always a story (or two or three) attached to it. The hope is that each time we create awareness of shame surrounding our stories and experiences, we can process and metabolize the shame and then move toward deeper, more embodied healing. You become the healed version of you as you dissolve the stories, and their effects lessen. The more you identify, see, and hear your stories and call them into question, the more they lose their hold. The accompanying messages that you are broken and not fixable, there's no hope for you, or that's "just the way you are" lose their grip on your psyche as you begin to see them as narratives that were just trying to make sense of what was happening to you in an attempt to keep the younger version of you feeling safe.

The good news is that this trauma is not permanent. Just as shame is cyclical, so is healing. Healing of trauma is available to you, me—everyone.

A few years ago, I adopted the mantra, "Shame has no power in the face of authenticity." I have discovered vulnerability plays a part in healing too. I have learned to lean into vulnerability and all the discomfort that comes with that commitment. I have experienced firsthand how the more authentic I am, the stronger I am and the more human I feel. Humans are fallible; every draft is a rough draft, and we find ourselves still revising even when we feel like the final draft deadline is upon us. There are no supposed to's, should be's, should haves, or ideal scenarios.

These are false concepts founded in shame, and they don't actually exist.

"Shame dies when stories are told in safe places."[18]

Stories, and the shame that often accompanies them, can be healed when shared with the hearts and souls of empathetic witnesses. The more vulnerable we are, the more we step into authenticity. The more authentic we are, the more we step into our power. The more powerful we are and feel, the more vulnerable we can continue to be.

And the more vulnerable we are in sharing our stories, the more we normalize that every human *has* stories that have shaped our shame and informed who we have been as we have lived within those stories.

It is sharing our stories that connects and binds us regardless of religion, faith, creed, skin color, race, ethnicity, background, sexuality, gender, or social demographics. These stories speak to this truth: we all are imperfect, fallible, messy, beautiful human beings. The more we share our stories, the more we empower each other to heal and dissolve our stories. The more healed we become, the more firmly we claim our sovereignty.

And finally, like sharing our stories, the experience of being human can be normalized. This foundational shift is available to anyone willing to do the work.

Nobody walks into a gym and expects their biceps and triceps to expand, contract, and strengthen on their own. We have to do the work. There is no way around it. And why would we want there to be?

---

[18] Ann Voskamp, @AnnVoscamp on *X*, October 3, 2016.

There is purpose, meaning, and exquisite beauty in the process of building and strengthening emotional muscles. Not enough value is placed on this journey, created one step at a time, especially for you and your personal evolution. Building your emotional muscles is a skill that can be honed and strengthened, just like it is with building physical muscles. It's not just a process of pushing through something hard or faking it til you make it.

It's called emotional resilience.

Though I haven't found a verified source, I love this quote I've seen attributed to Alecia Moore (aka P!nk):

> "Resilience is a muscle. Flex it enough and it will take less effort to get over the emotional punches each time."[19]

Additionally, I've found these to be powerful reminders of the importance of emotional resilience:

> "You may not control all the events that happen to you, but you can decide not to be reduced by them."[20]

> "Emotional resilience is when you are able to calm your frantic mind after encountering a negative experience. It is intrinsic motivation, an inner force by which we can hold ourselves through all the downsides of life.

---

[19] Quoted (but original source never stated) in the following: (1) Madhuleena Roy Chowdhury, BA, "What Is Emotional Resilience? (+6 proven Ways to Build It), PositivePsychology.com, January 22, 2019, https://positivepsychology.com/emotional-resilience/. (2) Fit Women's Weekly Facebook Post, September 13, 2017, https://www.facebook.com/photo.php?fbid=10155874419204589&id=80867644588&set=a.10150409636424589.

[20] Maya Angelou, *Letter to My Daughter*, Random House, 2008.

Just like other aspects of our persona, for example emotional intelligence and social intelligence, emotional resilience is a trait that is there since birth and continues to develop throughout life."[21]

Emotional resilience is one of the THREE pillars in my mini course:

Unlocking Your Voice™

Through patience (and doing the work myself), I have figured out the three pillars we need to turn up our volume.

1. Emotional resilience

2. Determining your core values

3. Identity work (learning your true identity through separating yourself from and then living a conscious life apart from your stories)

I learned to choose how much to share, with whom, how often, and where. I am in the driver's seat, not just in sharing my faith journey but in every aspect of my life.

There was a time when voicing the thoughts of my heart was out of the question—for sure on a public platform but also probably not even over lunch with a friend. I didn't know how to create the safety I needed to feel so I could speak vulnerably and openly.

I teach these three pillars in my mini course. I give you the keys you need to unlock and share your heart from a grounded, safe, confident place. When you do this life-changing and sometimes messy work, you witness your transformation in real time.

---

[21] Madhuleena Roy Chowdhury, B.A., "What is Emotional Resilience (+6 Proven Ways to Build It), January 22, 2019, positivepsychology.com

I have witnessed my own power simultaneously increase and become more deeply grounded, the more I have employed this work. This is what is available to you. Your energy—or power—will never be the same. Messy is beautiful. Embrace the messy.

Scan this QR code to access
the Unlocking Your Voice Mini Course:

use code TRANSPARENTSEE

To learn to unlock your voice and live Life Outside the Binary™* separate from your narratives will be one of your greatest gifts for your mental, emotional, spiritual, and physical self.

An exchange between Andrew McCarthy and Demi Moore on Hulu's *Brats* (released in 2024) is now one of my favorite examples of getting stuck inside our stories. Their conversation illustrates that even Hollywood actors are humans and can be trapped living inside a false narrative.

The subtitle of the June 14, 2024 RollingStone Magazine article by David Fear, "How Andrew McCarthy Made Peace with the Brat Pack—and then Made a Movie about It," states, "'Brats' is the star-turned-director's doc on the controversial label that defined then killed off an Eighties subgenre, and why he (Andrew) now embraces his connection with it."

Approximately fifty minutes into the documentary, producer Andrew McCarthy drives to the home of his friend Demi Moore, also considered an original member of the Hollywood "Brat Pack."

They sit out on Demi's backyard deck, and a candid, open discussion ensues. They talk of how being named members of the "Brat Pack" in a 1985 article written by David Blum in *New York Magazine* had an effect on each of them and their careers. Following is the transcript of Moore and McCarthy's conversation from *Brats*.

> Demi: I don't know if I took it as personal over time maybe than you did—or even the impact that you may have had from it.
>
> Andrew: I'm still wrangling with that notion of, like, I allowed that—even though I said I didn't.
>
> Demi: But it was like there was a belief that you were holding underneath, that you made that mean something about you, that then created a limitation in your expression. And that's, you know, and in—
>
> Andrew [*interrupting and laughing*]: Say that again! That's exactly right.
>
> [*Demi also laughs.*]
>
> Andrew [*smiling and laughing still*]: No, but that's exactly right. Fear was such a dominant part of my life when I was a kid. And it's still something I contend with on a daily basis, right? So—and my fear—I always felt like I was [*motioning toward his back with his left arm and pointing with his left hand*] being stabbed right between my shoulder blades by some unknown kind of thing. And that's

what I felt like when I first heard the term "Brat Pack."

Demi: I have a similar one in an old pattern. And mine was the rug being pulled out from under me. I look at everything is happening for us, not to us. You can't be selective with that. The fact that it came out to diminish us was also an opportunity to rise above and to say, 'No, I am much more than that. I am not, you know, for whatever the offensive part of being, kind of, seen as a brat.'

Andrew: For me, that's years in the process to come to that kind of thing. That's really just wise, you know? [*softly laughing*] That took me years to—because all I felt is, it was negative for so long, and—

Demi: But I think that that is a common part of our conditioning, is to see these things that have been, in a sense, what we hold as against-ness. It was like an against-ness to us. It was.

Andrew: Ooh, I like that—an "against-ness."

Demi: It was. But against-ness only provokes against-ness. And so when we hold things that way, we create that pattern.

Andrew: Totally.

Demi: Like that idea of being stabbed in the back is something you related to as something much earlier in your life.

Andrew: Yeah. So I'm predisposed to interpret it that way.

Demi: Not only that, you're predisposed to recreating it until you hit a point where you don't want to do that anymore.

Andrew [*smiling*]: Well, yeah. You go to enough therapy, and you kind of go—

Demi: And here you are. You're working through this just with that same purpose.

Andrew: And now here we are, doctor. Dr. Demi, listen to me! Listen.

[*Demi raises her arms victory style while laughing.*]

Andrew: I had ambition. And yet part of me—I have one hand that really wants something—and to this day, I have one hand that really wants something—and on the other hand I just want to go, "I just want to get the fuck out of here."

Demi: I'm so similar in that way. The other kind of story I had is wanting to hide and make myself small.

Andrew: I think when my life started to become more important than my career, I started to step back and have the perspective on the Brat Pack that it allowed me to do what we're talking about now, to see it as a good thing as opposed to—

Demi: Right.

Andrew: You know when I stopped pressing so hard, I think [I experienced] that shift which comes with age and/or failure.

Demi: The event is the event. What we make it mean is the value that it all of a sudden has. Does that—

Andrew: Yeah, I gave it so much power.

Demi: You gave it so—exactly. When you really look at that now we thought we were like so—

Andrew [*interjecting and laughing*]: And of course we thought we were so—like yeah—

Demi: —Grown up. But we were babies.

As Andrew leaves Demi's home, he shares his thoughts to the camera while driving.

> Things that happen to us when we're young, they're really intense and they go deep. Had the same thing—the Brat Pack—had happened when we were forty, we would've gone like "whatever dude," [but] 'cause you're young . . . you take it so personally 'cause you're not sure of yourself yet. So I think that article tapped into doubt and fears we had about ourselves. "Are we maybe undeserving of this? Are we this or that?" If it didn't touch something, it's like that old saying. "If it gets you, you got it." If it didn't touch some fear that we hadn't harbored about ourselves, it wouldn't have mattered.
>
> Was it touching truth? [*pauses*] It was touching fear, and fear is a powerful thing.[22]

Even movie stars go through the same human processes the rest of us do. The main difference is, they may have more exposure and visibility while doing so. They are on a proverbial stage for all to see their responses in real time. Whether their chosen words and actions are reactionary or purposeful, their responses, like ours,

---

[22] Movie quoted according to copyright fair use media law: https://www.pbs.org/standards/media-law-101/copyright-fair-use/#:~:text=Importantly%2C%20there%20is%20no%20set,use%3B%20each%20case%20is%20different.

reflect the narratives they don't even realize they are living in and acting from.

But, once we become aware of our false narratives, we must engage in the work of separating the stories from the facts to allow the emotions of our stories space to breathe. Then, we can do the work of processing and metabolizing the stories.

Ultimately, this process has the power to fundamentally change our recurring thought patterns, relationship with emotions, and how we perceive our actions, words, and subsequent outcomes viewed through the lenses of our stories. This is how we release ourselves from elements of the past that continue to have a hold on our psyche.

In other words, the strength our "predisposed" stories have on our self-concept has loosened, and the stories have dissipated. We are free.

This is transformation.

*Life Outside the Binary™: *When you experience an awakening and see for yourself the world is not all black and white. You choose which of your longheld stories align, and live outside the ones that don't.* ™ Scan this QR Code to join me in my free monthly group Life Outside the Binary™ First Friday's Free Coaching:

TransparentSEE

9

TRANSMUTATION
(change in form, nature, or substance)

I don't mind your odd behavior
It's the very thing I love
If you were an ice cream flavor
You would be my favorite one

My imagination sees you
Like a painting by Van Gogh
Starry nights and bright sunflowers
Follow you where you may go

———

You're a butterfly held captive
Small and safe in your cocoon
Go on, you can take your time (your time)
Time is said to heal all wounds

———

Like a lock without a key
Like a mystery without a clue
There is no me if I cannot have you

Oh, I've loved you from the start
In every single way
And more each passing day
You are brighter than the stars
Believe me when I say
It's not about your scars
It's all about your heart

> ~ *All about Your Heart,* Recorded by Mindy Gledhill,
> written Mindy Gledhill and Kendra Lowe

Before I could move forward in my journey, I had to look back. I don't mean *go* back and regress, but instead look, listen, feel, and learn from inside out. For me, that meant tending to my inner child, and sometimes my inner teenager or young adult. The Internal Family Systems (IFS) model refers to this as "parts work." We each have inner parts—sometimes called "sub-personalities"— that may be hurting, have unresolved trauma, and need to be seen and heard.

Most of us look outside for answers, and certainly that can be a good thing. But, if we are lost in old stories and stuck in outdated patterns—that at one time served a younger "part" or "sub-personality" but are now causing harm—then releasing and getting out of them and moving forward will be just out of our reach.

We can't get out of our own stories and patterns when we aren't aware of them, and if we're not aware of them, we will not be able to be the observer of them. Putting ourselves in the role of observer and purposely deciding if the patterns and narratives are helpful and needed or if causing pain and harm is the key to taking our power back.

It is possible to "parent" these parts, offering them the compassion and love they needed and did not receive. It is usually most effective to have a practitioner (i.e. coach or therapist) help facilitate this process. I have had a few practitioners to whom I am so grateful for facilitating the connections I've made to my younger self. I've had subsequent realizations of what she needed and didn't get and then offered that to her with love.

One of these connections happened Oct 7, 2023 while I was participating in Outside the Story with Coach (Scott) and Kim Job. I wrote about it in my journal:

> I feel young Meagan weeping inside for what she missed that she didn't even know she was looking for way back then 😔 .
>
> Big Meagan hurts for little Meagan. Why did I believe my worth and value really was based on a ring on my left finger (the younger the better) among other external things (accomplishments, callings), and boxes checked (serving a mission, temple marriage).
>
> Wow. I feel betrayed; I feel duped. But what I really feel is caged.
>
> And yet, I know where the swinging door is; it's not even locked. I'm afraid to even test the latch.
>
> What happens when you unlatch and swing the cage door open?
>
> I'm not used to still getting continuous reception with zero bars. 🪶
>
> If I go "off-grid," can I still find my way?

One of (if not THE) most important things I have done as I have been making my way is cultivating a relationship with myself. I had been taught to place more weight on the opinions of sources outside of me and not vice versa.

I remember this one particular day in fifth grade. My math teacher called on me to read the problem she had written on the chalkboard. I was embarrassed to be called on because I had to say, "I can't see it. I cannot see what is written on the board."

She suggested I may want to get my eyes checked; perhaps I needed glasses. I honestly don't recall if she said it in front of the class or waited until the hour was over, but I didn't care. I was so happy to learn that there might be a logical explanation and solution for my situation.

I thought she was going to be upset with me. I thought she might even shame me. However, she responded kindly, "That's OK," and then she asked another student to read.

I went home and told my mom what happened that day and what my teacher told me. Not too long after that, I was leaving the eye doctor with my new glasses.

It was like I was seeing the world for the first time. I couldn't believe what I had been missing out on, not because it wasn't there but because I couldn't see it before. I saw the trees, grass, sky, buildings, cars—everything—with such clarity that I thought it was magic.

How could some be able to see the world this sharply and clearly without the aid of lenses, and not others?! I couldn't imagine what that would be like.

At one point, I reasoned, I must have seen the world through that sharp and clear lens, assuming we are all born with 20/20 vision. But as the shape of my eye grew, the angle that light entered my cornea and reflected off the back of my eye was affected, changing the clarity of my vision—literally how I viewed the world.

As my vision slowly changed, I started to see things differently, but because it was so gradual, I didn't notice. I wasn't aware until it was staring me in the face that day in fifth grade math class, and then it was unmistakable that I was not seeing things the way others were seeing them. The reality became painfully obvious as I connected the dots in front of the whole class.

I have needed vision correction ever since. I have to actively work to provide myself the opportunity to see. I have myopia, which means I can see up close but not far away. So, my practitioner has prescribed lens correction to make up for what I cannot see on my own. It's not safe to drive without wearing my glasses because doing so would put me, my passengers, and those in cars around me at risk.

What helps me be a safer driver will not necessarily do the same for my loved ones, friends, or neighbors. If they were to use my glasses for driving, they would actually be at more risk. My lenses are meant to make up the difference and fill in the gaps of *my* vision, and mine alone. What works for me may not work for you, and that is OK.

What is needed in my life isn't necessarily what is needed in yours, and vice versa. The ability to see is unique to each individual.

Unlearning this idea of trusting sources and voices outside of me more than my own was hard work. It didn't seem intuitive nor come naturally at first. As my eyes opened and my "vision" changed, I had to continue to "try on new lenses." No one could do this for me.

Regardless of whether the Bible is a historical narrative or factual record, I love the symbolism of Eve's partaking of the apple. Actually, taking a bite of the fruit may have been symbolic, but the part about the eyes opening was real. At least, the concept and lesson is real.

Eve could only do this for herself. She couldn't do it for Adam and she could not force him to do what was needed (take the bite) in order to adjust his own "lenses."

It is the same for us; you cannot partake of my apple for me and vice versa. I cannot make you see the things I do or in the way I see them, nor can you for me.

As magical as my first pair of lenses were all the way back in fifth grade, I still believe in magic, just not the abracadabra, alakazam, hocus-pocus type.

During a writing session, Keira asked us, "Do you believe in magic?"

I wrote, "Yes, I believe in magic."

She persisted, "Why do you believe in magic?"

I wrote, "I guess that depends on one's perception of what magic is."

I decided that for me, magic is a mindset.

It is a goal to work toward.

It is a feeling we can embody.

I describe magic as mystery, intrigue, and belief in self. It's a belief in the forces around us, many of which we cannot see or fully understand in this present moment. It's a hope instilled in *what's next, what's beyond? And it trusts that Inner Voice to lead them there.*

This magical hope asks, "What's on the other side, and what's possible?"

This is the essence of transmutation.

10

TRANSCENDENCE

(existence or experience beyond the normal or physical level)

Lying in my bed
I hear the clock tick and think of you
Caught up in circles
Confusion is nothing new
Flashback, warm nights
Almost left behind
Suitcases of memories
Time after

Sometimes you picture me
I'm walking too far ahead
You're calling to me,
I can't hear what you've said
Then you say, "Go slow"
I fall behind
The second hand unwinds

———

After my picture fades
And darkness has turned to gray
Watching through windows
You're wondering if I'm okay
Secrets stolen from deep inside
And the drum beats out of time

If you're lost, you can look, and you will find me
Time after time
If you fall, I will catch you, I'll be waiting
Time after time

> ~ "Time after Time," Recorded by Cyndi Lauper, Written
> by Robert Hyman and Cyndi Lauper

While visiting my sister in Brinnon, WA one summer, I spotted a little bee outside my window and noted that it was in its natural habitat.

At one point, many many moons ago, the outdoors was the natural habitat for humans too. Is it still? When did *nature* become no longer my (or wo/man's) natural state of existing, living, and being?

In March of 2020, everything shut down worldwide during the Covid pandemic. The habitat that was familiar to humans ceased to exist at that moment in human history. Daily life, normal travel, and even regular visits with others came to an abrupt stop.

At the time, if you would have bet me $10k that I would get certified as a life coach, start a podcast, and publish a book—all about my experiences as a mom of a queer kiddo—I would have laughed. I would not have believed you were serious. I probably would have taken the bet because I did not see it in the cards. It was nowhere near my radar.

Here we are in 2024 and there has been a rebirth of daily life, travel, and in-person contact with friends, associates, and loved ones. I would be out $10k if I had taken that bet because all of those, and more, have come to fruition. You reading this book is evidence of that.

When I started my podcast in August 2022, I had zero clue that it would become a source of spiritual connection and sustenance for me. I didn't know it would be therapeutic, a balm to my soul. It took me about a year to realize that it was as much, or more, for me as it was for those who listened.

In episode 142, my guest Amy Jensen shared something I've never forgotten: "Questions are where transcendence is."[23]

My mind was blown.

If I had never leaned into the questioning of my understanding of gender, I would not have begun the journey to expand my view of God. I would have never transcended the previous understanding I had.

I'd known that the word for God, "Elohim," signified two—male and female—but I didn't really know what that meant.

I always understood there to be a very black and white binary of human existence: male and female. Anything outside of that in humans or in nature was something that was a mutation and needed "fixing" until it was back to being as close as possible to "the norm."

I've learned a lot about this concept of "the norm." I've learned to question it. Is it a set standard against which we must all compare ourselves and which we must aspire to achieve or reflect?

No. A norm is a made up story, or perhaps a lie we've been given, that has been passed down for generations.

We aren't required to accept every offering.

---

[23] *Beyond the Shadow of Doubt* podcast, Episode 142, Embracing the Question where Transcendence Is with Amy Jensen."

Even "set standard" is ambiguous, as it is relative to whomever you might be conversing with or within whichever community you may dwell.

For me (and maybe for you too), it begs the questions:

Which era, generation, ethnicity, religion, culture, nationality, language (I could go on) is "lucky" enough to have the so-called established norm?

And if such a society or group exists, then what do we do about clownfish?

I learned God is in the gender fluid clownfish that shift their gender according to the needs of the environment, and in the male seahorse carrying embryos to term in his pouch.

God is in the baby elephant that stays faithfully by its stuck-in-the-mud mother's side until rescue workers help them get out.

God is in the mother cat that not only tolerates but takes in, cares for, and grooms young ducklings.

And God is in the female Great Dane nursing orphaned baby Chihuahuas.

God is in the donkey that wandered away from its owner's property and more than five years later was spotted by his owners in a pasture after having been adopted by a herd of deer.

God is in the human born with male chromosomes and female body parts and the one born with female body parts and feels more masculine on the inside (transgender). I see God in the human born with a uterus, who also has undescended testes that were previously assumed to be ovaries (intersex). These are real people living real lives, and they have real experiences and real feelings. Science has assigned names to their "conditions" because that is what science does to try to make sense of the world. The default seems to be to fear when something is unknown.

God is in the conjoined twins born sharing a brain, or heart and lungs; cases of this have been documented in many different countries across the world.

God is in the creatures of the deep—the unusual creatures that only exist at subzero temperatures.

Speaking of the deep, where does the earth's crust end and the magma begin and eventually arrive at the core, however many miles below the earth's surface?

Where does the *crust* even begin? Is it the layers of soil that make up my vegetable garden? Or is it below the water table?

Does it end once it reaches the edge of the solid surface and begins to touch the atmosphere—the air that we breathe?

Where does the air we breathe end?

I see God even in that liminal part of the atmosphere where an astronaut passes the clouds, still within Earth's reach and not quite yet in the vast expanse of space. What is the purpose of that in-between place?

Surely it serves a purpose.

It's a transition, a place to gradually move outside of Earth's gravitational pull toward the weightless unknown. The force required to push through that gravitational pull is so great that only rocket-propelled machinery can power to the other side.

To exist on "the other side" is no small task. It requires Herculean effort.

On April 8, 2024 I saw God all along the path of totality that stretched from Mexico to Dallas to the Midwest and on to New York and Montreal. Old and young, black and white, gay and straight, male and female and everyone in between along that path experienced the same event in those precious few minutes.

The moon started to take its place, passing slowly in front of the sun from the southwest starting at approximately 1:00 p.m. Central Standard Time. It wasn't until about 1:30 p.m. that a significant change in brightness could be detected. At approximately 1:40 p.m. the moon took center stage, and applause and cheers erupted throughout my neighborhood as totality set in.

IT. WAS. AWESOME.

We were all sitting in the bosom of Mother Earth, looking up at the same Father Sky that was holding the same moon and the same sun. There was a peaceful hush that settled in as the light dimmed, the darkness grew, and the moment of totality began.

All went calm, and the ring of totality was bright. The magic of the moment was unmistakable.

For four glorious minutes we were encircled by a 360-degree sunset, and it was as though all of nature was reverencing this historic event with a sacred stillness.

Words really cannot adequately describe it.

During these four minutes, we were able to remove the special eclipse glasses and look straight at the sun, now a ring of totality. It shone like a halo and was other-worldly. Although there was a shadow cast from the eclipse, the ring of totality was created by the light behind the shadow, cast by the moon passing in front of the sun. It made it evident that there was **still light**. The light had not simply vanished. The light of the sun was still peeking out from behind the moon.

This moment where all of Mother Nature and Father Sky aligned was a reminder of a simple truth—there exists something bigger than all of us. So much bigger. Profoundly bigger.

From the vantage point of space, we are all unified in that we are all part of the same giant human family. There are no visible country or state boundary lines; those are created by man. All along the path of totality, the cheers of our fellow humans were the same, celebrating this same glorious event occurring in the same great universe.

It was absolutely unforgettable.

I experienced it with my two kids. They, too, felt the ethereal and spiritual nature of the event, especially my youngest. He verbalized how his heart filled with joy, his eyes with tears, his mind with awe. His soul was forever stirred, eternally moved, profoundly touched.

No matter our skin color, heritage, orientation, or marital status, we all know what it feels like to experience being human. The specific circumstances will not be the same, but the hunger, thirst, fatigue, joy, and wonderment are universal experiences.

At 1:44 p.m. we had to put our glasses back on as the moon began to leave the spotlight at center stage. The ring of totality began to fade.

By 2:15 p.m. the moon had moved on (probably to Kansas City), and the sun was shining like usual.

There was no single point in the process where it was only dark or only blindingly bright. As a matter of fact, the day started out cloudy. We weren't even sure we would get to see the eclipse with the clouds getting in the way.

But not only did they part and allow us to witness totality, the play of light muted by and reflecting off of the breaking clouds created a heavenly backdrop.

My good friend Becky Belnap is also a parent of a transgender child. I interviewed her on my podcast, and I'll never forget what she shared there: "I'd rather live in a world of sunrises and sunsets."[24] Amen, Becky. We experience those heavenly backdrops at least twice a day. Without the spectrum of light to darkness, cloudiness to clear skies, we would not have been able to experience the eclipse nor would we experience our daily sunrises and sunsets.

---

[24] *Beyond the Shadow of Doubt* podcast, Episode 114, "I Want to Live in a World with Sunrises and Sunsets with Becky Belnap."

What if our understanding of gender and sexuality is limited by a color line of only black and white, while just below the surface lies a brilliant spectrum, a heavenly backdrop of sorts, waiting to be seen and to shine? This spectrum already exists, with colors we've yet to see, at least in the United States. Some peoples and cultures have seen this spectrum, and their histories notate it.

The Finnish have long acknowledged fluidity of gender in their use of language.

> "Hän" is the gender-neutral Finnish personal pronoun that treats everyone equally.
>
> In the Finnish language, personal pronouns (words used as substitutes for a person's name, such as he and she) do not specify whether the person discussed is a woman or a man. One word—hän—refers to women, men, and people of other genders alike. . . .
>
> Similar gender-neutral personal pronouns are typical of languages related to Finnish, Finno-Urgic languages . . . and is also a feature of some other languages, such as Sino-Tibetan, Altaic and Bantu languages.[25]

Some native cultures, such as Hawaiian and Samoan, also have a history of acknowledging three and even four genders. According to an article from manoanow.org, a student run organization,

> In Hawaiian or Kanaka Maoli culture, gender is not a binary concept. Kānaka Maoli acknowledged those who did not simply identify as male or female. The third gender is the māhū, or "the in-between."

---

[25] https://finland.fi/han/article/

This Hawaiian term is used to characterize someone who embodies both kāne (male) and wahine (female) spirit. Many other Pacific Islander cultures share this understanding of a third gender. In Tongan, the term is "fakaleiti," and, in Sāmoan, the term is "fa'afafine."[26]

An article from the Natural History Museum of Los Angeles County shares the following:

Many third gender individuals hold integral roles within societies and are well respected for their strength, hard work, and ability to discuss taboo topics. On the island of Samoa, there are four recognized cultural genders: female, male, fa'afafine, and fa'afatama. Fa'afafine and fa'afatama are fluid gender roles that move between male and female worlds. These third and fourth gender groups tend to care for elders in the community and educate others about sex, a topic considered taboo in public conversations for male and female genders.[27]

Isabella Thurston of the Canadian-based Indigenous Foundation wrote the following:

The **concept** of Two-Spirit folks existed **well before** the arrival of European settlers on Turtle Island. Indigenous individuals who identified as **Two-Spirit** folks were seen as **gifted** and **honoured** in their community because they carried two spirits with them, both male and female. 2S folks were often the **healers**, **medicine**

---

[26] Meldrick Ravida, "The Māhū," *Ka Leo, The Voice of Hawaii*, February 11, 2018
[27] "Beyond Gender: Indigenous Perspectives, Fa'afafine and Fa'afatama," September 1, 2020

people, and **visionaries** within their given community and they were foundational members of their culture. Much of this can be attributed to the "double vision" 2S people are gifted with, being able to see both through the masculine and feminine lens.[28]

The definition of the prefix "trans" means "to cross over, the other side of." In each of these previous examples, the other side is

rare,

exquisite,

unique,

uncommon,

heartfelt,

it leaves its own footprint,

is deeply personal, and

is evidence of the Divinity of all creations.

It is truly breathtaking.

When I was in college, I had a boss who had been a pilot in the Air Force. He recounted to me the details of a flight he made across the US. He started at sunset on the East Coast and headed to California. The beauty he described was marvelous. He and his copilot followed the sun the entire flight; it seemingly never set. They witnessed a spectacular show put on by Mother Nature and Father Sky.

This begs the question: where does the sunset end? Or does it end?

Somewhere in the world, there is always a sunset. Always.

---

[28] https://www.theindigenousfoundation.org/articles/the-history-of-two-spirit-folks

Somewhere in the world, the rays from the great burning ball of gases are bouncing off a millennia of dust, particles, and clouds creating colors only you can see.

The naked human eye is what makes the viewing of color possible. There is a precise moment when a light ray passes through the lens, hits the cornea, refracts off it, passes back out, and absorbs or hits the object in focus, and the colors of the sunset, sunrise, or rainbow appear.

Does the rainbow exist if there is no human eye to witness it?

The enormous waves of blue shift, and depending on the conditions—weather, clouds, sunlight, time of day, surroundings, air quality—you may see a color of blue so exquisite while the person next to you sees an equally exquisite yet different shade of blue.

How can we tell the "true" shade? Is there a way to know for sure what *exact* color of blue the sky is without actually having another person's set of eyes?

I propose the answer is no.

Does it matter?

I say it matters to the one experiencing it; in fact, that is precisely for whom it is intended. Everything isn't meant for everyone. Whatever you experience, others around you get to witness the joy and awe you are experiencing. But make no mistake, witnessing is their only role. They do not get to *tell* you what you are witnessing. That is something only your soul gets the privilege to whisper to and teach you.

It is miraculous to watch and witness those around us transcend the metaphorical mortal gravitational pull and figuratively touch the finger of God.

See . . .

your spouse,

your bff,

your parents,

your family,

your loved ones and

your faith community

as they release their grip on

judgment, shame, supposed to's and should haves,

and clasp anew a deep, abiding, unconditional love.

And you consciously choose to let them go as you surrender to the unknown what you may not fully understand, but you have a willing, listening, open heart.

It's spiritual heart surgery by the most talented, perfect (whole) Surgeon.

I'm talking the kind of love that builds and births under the atmospheric pressure, pushes you to the brink of your gravitational boundaries where you find the ashes and residue of prejudice, bigotry, and bias because they have been consumed by fire in the transition from Earth to sky to atmosphere to the great universe.

This is transcendence.

EPILOGUE

I am unwritten
Can't read my mind
I'm undefined
I'm just beginning
The pen's in my hand
Ending unplanned

Staring at the blank page before you
Open up the dirty window
Let the sun illuminate the words that you could not
find

Reaching for something in the distance
So close you can almost taste it
Release your inhibitions
Feel the rain on your skin
No one else can feel it for you
Only you can let it in
No one else, no one else
Can speak the words on your lips
Drench yourself in words unspoken
Live your life with arms wide open
Today is where your book begins
The rest is still unwritten

Oh, oh, oh

I break tradition
Sometimes my tries are outside the lines
We've been conditioned to not make mistakes
But I can't live that way

Staring at the blank page before you
Open up the dirty window
Let the sun illuminate the words that you could not
find

Reaching for something in the distance
So close you can almost taste it
Release your inhibitions
Feel the rain on your skin
No one else can feel it for you
Only you can let it in
No one else, no one else
Can speak the words on your lips
Drench yourself in words unspoken
Live your life with arms wide open
Today is where your book begins
The rest is still unwritten

~ "Unwritten," recorded by Natasha Bedingfield,
written by Danielle A. Brisebois, Natasha Anne
Bedingfield, and Wayne Steven Jr Rodrigues

Dear Reader,

May the opening of my heart and sharing of my ponderings along my journey create a spark in your soul.

May this spark, when fanned with compassion, interest, and curiosity burst into flames that will exponentially grow into an all-consuming fire throughout humanity. And may this fire create the warmth and heart-to-heart connection that can only come from sharing our sacred stories, which are our truth.

May you seek the brilliance and guidance of the sun which will illuminate the words perhaps unseen or unknown to you now, but assuredly—**they are already in existence.**

May you reflect and remember that truly no one else can speak your book, and feel, taste, and tell your story. No one else can open your arms, heart, and soul wide open but YOU.

YOU are the captain of your vessel, the master of your seas. Break tradition, open up the dirty windows, try outside ALL. THE. LINES. Make mistakes. Make lots of them!

As Bob Ross, the Happy Painter, said, "There are no mistakes, just happy accidents."

Embrace you and your life with all the rough seas, in all the messiness, for this is where beauty is also found.

We are human beings, not human doings. This is BEING.

Don't be stingy with your storytelling. May you tell them all, tell them wide, and tell them freely.

With that, I give you my heart. May you guard it and treat it with the love and compassion you do your own.

Love,

Enjoy Exclusive Bonuses!

Thank you for reading *TransparentSEE*.
As a special thank you,
I've created exclusive bonuses just for you.

How to Access Your Book Bonuses

Simply scan the QR code below with your phone to
unlock your special resources:

TRANSPARENTSEE BONUS
CONTENT & SOURCES CITED